P9-CJX-793

WeightWatchers®
PointsPlus®™

Fresh, Fabulous
Fast

140 RECIPES ALL UNDER 30 MINUTES

About ⦅WeightWatchers®

Weight Watchers International, Inc., is the world's leading provider of weight-management services, operating globally through a network of company-owned and franchise operations. Weight Watchers holds nearly 50,000 weekly meetings worldwide, at which members receive group support and education about healthful eating patterns, behavior modification, and physical activity. Weight-loss and weight-management results vary by individual. We recommend that you attend Weight Watchers meetings to benefit from the supportive environment you find there and follow the comprehensive Weight Watchers program, which includes a food plan, an activity plan, and a behavioral component. In addition, Weight Watchers offers a wide range of products, publications, and programs for people interested in weight loss and weight control. For the Weight Watchers meeting nearest you, call **1-800-651-6000**. For information about bringing Weight Watchers to your workplace, call **1-800-8AT-WORK**. Also visit us at our Web site, WeightWatchers.com, and look for **Weight Watchers Magazine** at your newsstand or in your meeting room.

*Lemon-Basil Tofu
with Pasta and
Zucchini, page 53*

WEIGHT WATCHERS PUBLISHING GROUP

EDITORIAL DIRECTOR Nancy Gagliardi

CREATIVE DIRECTOR Ed Melnitsky

PRODUCTION MANAGER Alan Biederman

PHOTO EDITOR Deborah Hardt

MANAGING EDITOR Sarah Wharton

EDITORIAL ASSISTANT Katerina Gkionis

FOOD EDITOR Eileen Runyan

EDITOR Jackie Mills, MS, RD

NUTRITION CONSULTANT Jacqueline Kroon, MS, RD

RECIPE DEVELOPERS Jean Galton, Debby Goldsmith, Lori Longbotham, Maureen Luchejko, Rick Rodgers

PHOTOGRAPHER Iain Bagwell

FOOD STYLIST Simon Andrews

PROP STYLIST Paige Hicks

ART DIRECTOR Ellen Swandiak

ON THE COVER:

left: Pecan-Crusted Chicken with Cilantro Slaw, p. 30

center: Lamb Kebabs with Yogurt-Mint Sauce, p. 74

right: Greek Chicken with Peppers and Pasta, p. 132

Copyright © 2011 Weight Watchers International, Inc.
Nothing may be reprinted in whole or in part without permission from the publisher.
Editorial and art produced by W/W Twentyfirst Corp., 11 Madison Avenue, New York, NY 10010.
WEIGHT WATCHERS is a registered trademark of Weight Watchers International, Inc.
SKU #11185 Printed in the USA

About Our Recipes

While losing weight isn't only about what you eat, Weight Watchers realizes the critical role it plays in your success and overall good health. That's why our philosophy is to offer great-tasting, easy recipes that are nutritious as well as delicious. We make every attempt to use wholesome ingredients and to ensure that our recipes fall within the recommendations of the U.S. Dietary Guidelines for Americans for a diet that promotes health and reduces the risk for disease. If you have special dietary needs, consult with your health-care professional for advice on a diet that is best for you, then adapt these recipes to meet your specific nutritional needs.

To achieve these good-health goals and get the maximum satisfaction from the foods you eat, we suggest you keep the following information in mind while preparing our recipes:

THE *PointsPlus*™ PROGRAM AND GOOD NUTRITION

■ Recipes in this book have been developed for Weight Watchers members who are following the *PointsPlus* program. *PointsPlus* values are given for each recipe. They're assigned based on the amount of protein (grams), carbohydrates (grams), fat (grams), and fiber (grams) contained in a single serving of a recipe.

■ Recipes include approximate nutritional information; they are analyzed for Calories (Cal), Total Fat, Saturated Fat (Sat Fat), Trans Fat, Cholesterol (Chol), Sodium (Sod), Carbohydrates (Carb), Sugar, Dietary Fiber (Fib), Protein (Prot), and Calcium (Calc). The nutritional values are calculated by registered dietitians, using nutrition analysis software.

■ Substitutions made to the ingredients will alter the per-serving nutritional information and may affect the *PointsPlus* value.

■ Our recipes meet Weight Watchers Good Health Guidelines for eating lean proteins and fiber-rich whole grains, and having at least five servings of vegetables and fruits and two servings of low-fat or fat-free dairy products a day, while limiting your intake of saturated fat, sugar, and sodium.

■ Health agencies recommend limiting sodium intake. To stay in line with this recommendation we keep sodium levels in our recipes reasonably low; to boost flavor, we often include fresh herbs or a squeeze of citrus instead of salt. If you don't have to restrict your sodium, feel free to add a touch more salt as desired.

■ In the recipes, a green triangle (▲) indicates Weight Watchers® Power Foods.

▲ Healthy Extra suggestions have a *PointsPlus* value of 0 unless otherwise stated.

■ Recipes that work with the Simply Filling technique are listed on page 223. Find more details about this technique at your meeting.

For information about the science behind lasting weight loss and more, please visit **WeightWatchers.com/science.**

READ THIS FIRST: SHOPPING FOR INGREDIENTS

As you learn to eat healthier and add more Power Foods to your meals, remember these tips for choosing foods wisely:

LEAN MEATS AND POULTRY Purchase lean meats and poultry, and trim them of all visible fat before cooking. When poultry is cooked with the skin on, we recommend removing the skin before eating. Nutritional information for recipes that include meat, poultry, and fish is based on cooked, skinless boneless portions (unless otherwise stated), with the fat trimmed.

SEAFOOD Whenever possible, our recipes call for seafood that is sustainable and deemed the most healthful for human consumption so that your choice of seafood is not only good for the oceans but also good for you. For more information about the best seafood choices and to download a pocket guide, go to **environmentaldefensefund.org** or **montereybayaquarium.org**. For information about mercury and seafood go to **weightwatchers.com**.

PRODUCE For best flavor, maximum nutrient content, and the lowest prices, buy fresh, local produce, such as vegetables, leafy greens, and fruits in season. Rinse them thoroughly before using and keep a supply of cut-up vegetables and fruits in your refrigerator for convenient, healthy snacks.

WHOLE GRAINS Explore your market for whole-grain products such as whole wheat and whole-grain breads and pastas, brown rice, bulgur, barley, cornmeal, whole wheat couscous, oats, and quinoa to enjoy with your meals.

PREPARATION AND MEASURING

READ THE RECIPE Take a couple of minutes to read through the ingredients and directions before you start to prepare a recipe. This will prevent you from discovering midway through that you don't have an important ingredient or that a recipe requires several hours of marinating. And it's also a good idea to assemble all ingredients and utensils within easy reach before you begin a recipe.

WEIGHING AND MEASURING The success of any recipe depends on accurate weighing and measuring. The effectiveness of the Weight Watchers program and the accuracy of the nutritional analysis depend on correct measuring as well. Use the following techniques:

• Weigh food such as meat, poultry, and fish on a food scale.

• To measure liquids, use a standard glass or plastic measuring cup placed on a level surface. For amounts less than ¼ cup, use standard measuring spoons.

• To measure dry ingredients, use metal or plastic measuring cups that come in ¼-, ⅓-, ½-, and 1-cup sizes. Fill the appropriate cup and level it with the flat edge of a knife or spatula. For amounts less than ¼ cup, use standard measuring spoons.

**Fig-Glazed Pork Chops
with Green Beans, page 114**

Contents

30 MIN

fast

*Got half an hour?
Then you've got time
to make one of these
fresh, flavorful main
dishes any night
of the week. Basic
pantry staples and
streamlined cooking
techniques ensure
that these meals are
on the table fast.*

Harissa-Spiced Sirloin with Raisin Couscous

SERVES 4

2 tablespoons harissa

2 teaspoons olive oil

1 teaspoon dried oregano

½ teaspoon salt

▲ 1 (1-pound) boneless sirloin steak, trimmed

▲ 1 cup reduced-sodium chicken broth

2 tablespoons lemon juice

▲ 1 cup whole wheat couscous

1 tablespoon golden raisins

1 tablespoon pine nuts, toasted

1 tablespoon chopped fresh mint

1 Combine harissa, 1 teaspoon of the oil, the oregano, and ¼ teaspoon of the salt in small bowl; spread over both sides of steak. Let stand at room temperature 10 minutes.

2 Spray large ridged grill pan with nonstick spray and set over medium-high heat. Add steak and cook until instant-read thermometer inserted into center of steak registers 145°F for medium-rare, 3–4 minutes on each side. Transfer steak to cutting board and let stand 5 minutes.

3 Meanwhile, bring broth, lemon juice, and remaining 1 teaspoon oil and ¼ teaspoon salt to boil in medium saucepan; add couscous, raisins, pine nuts, and mint. Cover and remove from heat. Let stand 5 minutes, then fluff with fork. Cut steak across grain into 12 slices. Serve with couscous.

PER SERVING *(3 slices steak + ¾ cup couscous):* *215 grams, 317 Cal, 10 g Total Fat, 2 g Sat Fat, 0 g Trans Fat, 49 mg Chol, 485 mg Sod, 27 g Carb, 2 g Sugar, 4 g Fib, 32 g Prot, 39 mg Calc.*

Harissa-Spiced Sirloin with Raisin Couscous

Gaucho Steak with Roasted Poblanos

▲ **4 poblano peppers**

▲ **1 (1-pound) flank steak, trimmed**

2 garlic cloves, minced

¾ teaspoon ground cumin

½ teaspoon salt

2 teaspoons olive oil

▲ **1 large red onion, sliced**

2 tablespoons chopped fresh cilantro

Juice of 1 lime

2 tablespoons crumbled queso fresco or feta cheese

F.Y.I.

If poblano peppers are unavailable, you can **substitute green bell peppers**. Omit step 1 and cook two thinly sliced green bell peppers with the onion in step 3.

---

1 Preheat broiler. Spray baking sheet with nonstick spray. Place poblanos on baking sheet and broil 5 inches from heat, turning occasionally, until lightly charred on all sides, about 5 minutes. Place poblanos in paper bag and fold closed. Let steam 5 minutes. When cool enough to handle, peel poblanos, discard seeds, and cut into ½-inch strips.

2 Meanwhile, rub steak with 1 of the garlic cloves, the cumin, and ¼ teaspoon of the salt. Spray large nonstick ridged grill pan with nonstick spray and set over medium-high heat. Add steak and cook until instant-read thermometer inserted into side of steak registers 145°F for medium, 3–4 minutes on each side. Transfer to cutting board and let stand 5 minutes.

3 At same time, heat oil in large nonstick skillet over medium-high heat. Add onion and remaining garlic clove and ¼ teaspoon salt. Cook, stirring occasionally, until softened and browned, about 5 minutes. Add poblanos, cilantro, and lime juice and cook until heated through, about 1 minute.

4 Cut steak across grain into 12 slices. Place steak on platter; top with poblano mixture and sprinkle with cheese.

6 PointsPlus® value ™ Per Serving

PER SERVING *(3 slices steak, ½ cup poblano mixture, + ½ tablespoon cheese): 180 grams, 261 Cal, 11 g Total Fat, 4 g Sat Fat, 0 g Trans Fat, 44 mg Chol, 359 mg Sod, 14 g Carb, 2 g Sugar, 5 g Fib, 27 g Prot, 64 mg Calc.*

Grilled Beef Kebabs with Tomato-Feta Salsa

▲ **1 pound beef sirloin, trimmed and cut into 16 chunks**

▲ **2 scallions, thinly sliced**

1 teaspoon dried oregano

1 teaspoon olive oil

$\frac{1}{2}$ teaspoon salt

▲ **2 tomatoes, chopped**

▲ **$\frac{1}{2}$ English (seedless) cucumber, diced**

1 shallot, finely chopped

Zest and juice of 1 lime

2 tablespoons chopped fresh mint

2 tablespoons crumbled reduced-fat feta cheese

1 Spray grill rack with nonstick spray. Preheat grill to medium-high or prepare medium-high fire.

2 Toss together beef, scallions, oregano, oil, and $\frac{1}{4}$ teaspoon of the salt in large bowl. Let stand at room temperature 10 minutes. Thread beef onto 4 (8-inch) metal skewers. Place kebabs on grill rack and grill until instant-read thermometer inserted into piece of beef registers 145°F for medium, 3–4 minutes on each side.

3 Meanwhile, to make salsa, combine tomatoes, cucumber, shallot, lime zest and juice, mint, and remaining $\frac{1}{4}$ teaspoon salt in medium bowl. Top with feta. Serve kebabs with salsa.

5 PointsPlus® value ™
Per Serving

PER SERVING *(1 kebab + $\frac{1}{2}$ cup salsa): 227 grams, 203 Cal, 7 g Total Fat, 2 g Sat Fat, 0 g Trans Fat, 51 mg Chol, 410 mg Sod, 6 g Carb, 3 g Sugar, 2 g Fib, 28 g Prot, 58 mg Calc.*

▲ *Healthy Extra*

Add 1 cup fresh or thawed frozen corn kernels to the salsa. The per-serving **PointsPlus** value will increase by **1**.

*Asian Beef Sliders with
Pickled Cucumbers*

Asian Beef Sliders with Pickled Cucumbers

SERVES 8

▲ **2 Kirby cucumbers, thinly sliced**

▲ **1 small red onion, thinly sliced**

3 tablespoons rice vinegar

1 tablespoon minced peeled fresh ginger

1 tablespoon chopped fresh mint

¼ teaspoon red pepper flakes

▲ **1 ¼ pounds ground lean beef (7% fat or less)**

▲ **¼ cup thinly sliced scallions**

2 teaspoons chili-garlic sauce

¼ teaspoon salt

1 ½ teaspoons wasabi powder

1 ½ teaspoons water

¼ cup low-fat mayonnaise

8 (3-inch) mini sandwich buns (1 ½ ounces each), split

1 Spray grill rack with nonstick spray. Preheat grill to medium-high or prepare medium-high fire.

2 Toss together cucumbers, onion, vinegar, ginger, mint, and pepper flakes in medium bowl; let stand 10 minutes.

3 Combine beef, scallions, chili-garlic sauce, and salt in large bowl and mix well. With damp hands, form mixture into 8 patties. Place patties on grill rack and grill until instant-read thermometer inserted into side of each burger registers 160°F for medium, 4–5 minutes on each side.

4 Meanwhile, to make dressing, stir together wasabi powder and water in small bowl until smooth; whisk in mayonnaise. Spread cut sides of buns with dressing. Place burgers in buns and top evenly with cucumber mixture.

 5 PointsPlus value Per Serving

PER SERVING *(1 burger): 128 grams, 239 Cal, 8 g Total Fat, 3 g Sat Fat, 0 g Trans Fat, 51 mg Chol, 387 mg Sod, 24 g Carb, 5 g Sugar, 2 g Fib, 18 g Prot, 52 mg Calc.*

F.Y.I.

Wasabi powder is made from Japanese horseradish and gives foods a fiery flavor. If it is not available, you can make a spicy mayonnaise for these sandwiches by adding hot sauce to taste to the low-fat mayonnaise.

Beef and Mushroom Ragu with Polenta

SERVES 4

- ▲ **1 pound beef sirloin, trimmed and thinly sliced**
- **½ teaspoon salt**
- **2 teaspoons canola oil**
- ▲ **1 (10-ounce) package sliced cremini mushrooms**
- ▲ **1 onion, sliced**
- **2 garlic cloves, minced**
- ▲ **1 (14 ½-ounce) can diced tomatoes**
- ▲ **¾ cup reduced-sodium beef broth**
- **½ cup dry red wine**
- **1 teaspoon dried thyme**
- **½ cup chopped fresh basil**
- **2 cups water**
- ▲ **½ cup instant polenta**

1 Sprinkle beef with ¼ teaspoon of the salt. Heat 1 teaspoon of the oil in large nonstick skillet over medium-high heat. Add beef in batches and cook, turning occasionally, until lightly browned, 3–4 minutes. Transfer beef to plate.

2 Heat remaining 1 teaspoon oil in same skillet over medium-high heat. Add mushrooms, onion, and garlic. Cook, stirring occasionally, until vegetables are tender, about 5 minutes. Add tomatoes, broth, wine, thyme, and remaining ¼ teaspoon salt; bring to boil. Reduce heat and simmer, stirring occasionally, until sauce is slightly thickened, 6–8 minutes. Return beef to skillet; heat through. Remove from heat; stir in basil. Keep warm.

3 Meanwhile, to make polenta, bring water to boil in large saucepan. Slowly pour in polenta in thin, steady stream, whisking constantly. Cook, whisking constantly, until thick and creamy, about 5 minutes. Divide polenta evenly among 4 serving plates; top each serving evenly with ragu.

8 PointsPlus® value

Per Serving

PER SERVING (1 cup ragu + ½ cup polenta): 395 grams, 352 Cal, 9 g Total Fat, 3 g Sat Fat, 0 g Trans Fat, 51 mg Chol, 783 mg Sod, 28 g Carb, 8 g Sugar, 3 g Fib, 33 g Prot, 110 mg Calc.

Pressure Cooker Pepper Pot Stew

SERVES 4

2 teaspoons olive oil

▲ 1 pound bottom round steak, trimmed and cut into 1-inch chunks

▲ 1 onion, chopped

3 garlic cloves, minced

▲ 2 carrots, cut into ½-inch slices

▲ 2 parsnips, peeled and cut into 1-inch chunks

▲ 2 cups reduced-sodium beef broth

½ cup dry red wine

1 teaspoon habanero pepper sauce

½ teaspoon ground allspice

½ teaspoon salt

4 teaspoons cornstarch

3 tablespoons cold water

▲ 1 cup frozen green peas, thawed

1 Heat oil in 6-quart pressure cooker over medium-high heat. Add steak, onion, and garlic and cook, stirring occasionally, until beef is lightly browned, about 3 minutes. Add carrots, parsnips, broth, wine, pepper sauce, allspice, and salt.

2 Lock lid in place and increase heat to high. Bring cooker to high pressure, following manufacturer's directions. Reduce heat and cook at high pressure 15 minutes.

3 Place pot in sink and run cold water over lid to bring pressure down quickly. When pressure indicator releases, remove pot from sink and unlock lid, following manufacturer's directions.

4 Whisk together cornstarch and water in small bowl until smooth. Add cornstarch mixture and peas to pressure cooker. Cook over medium-high heat, stirring constantly, until sauce is thickened and peas are heated through, about 1 minute.

8 PointsPlus® value ™ Per Serving

PER SERVING *(1 ½ cups): 408 grams, 372 Cal, 10 g Total Fat, 3 g Sat Fat, 0 g Trans Fat, 88 mg Chol, 432 mg Sod, 30 g Carb, 10 g Sugar, 7 g Fib, 35 g Prot, 79 mg Calc.*

Sun-Dried Tomato and Basil Stuffed Pork

SERVES 4

▲ **1 (1-pound) pork tenderloin, trimmed and cut on diagonal into 8 slices**

½ teaspoon salt

▲ **16 dry-packed sun-dried tomatoes**

16 fresh basil leaves

4 (½-ounce) slices reduced-fat Havarti cheese, halved

2 teaspoons olive oil

1 shallot, finely chopped

2 teaspoons all-purpose flour

▲ **½ cup reduced-sodium chicken broth**

¼ cup dry vermouth

2 teaspoons lemon juice

1 teaspoon chopped fresh rosemary

1 Place pork slices in single layer between 2 sheets of wax paper. With meat mallet or rolling pin, lightly pound each slice to ¼-inch thickness. Sprinkle pork with ¼ teaspoon of the salt. Top each slice with 2 sun-dried tomatoes, 2 basil leaves, and 1 piece Havarti. Starting from short sides, roll up pork and secure with wooden toothpicks.

2 Heat 1 teaspoon of the oil in large nonstick skillet over medium-high heat. Add pork rolls and cook, turning often, until lightly browned, 4–5 minutes. Transfer rolls to plate.

3 To make sauce, heat remaining 1 teaspoon oil in same skillet over medium-high heat. Add shallot and cook, stirring occasionally, until softened, 1–2 minutes. Sprinkle shallot with flour; cook, stirring constantly, 1 minute. Whisk in broth, vermouth, lemon juice, rosemary, and remaining ¼ teaspoon salt; bring to boil, stirring until sauce bubbles and thickens.

4 Return pork rolls and any accumulated juices to skillet. Reduce heat and simmer, uncovered, until pork rolls are heated through, 2–3 minutes. Remove toothpicks before serving. Serve rolls with sauce.

PER SERVING *(2 rolls + about 2 tablespoons sauce): 210 grams, 248 Cal, 10 g Total Fat, 4 g Sat Fat, 0 g Trans Fat, 75 mg Chol, 664 mg Sod, 7 g Carb, 3 g Sugar, 1 g Fib, 28 g Prot, 125 mg Calc.*

Sun-Dried Tomato and Basil Stuffed Pork

Grilled Pork Tenderloin with Chipotle-Peach Glaze

2 teaspoons chili powder

2 teaspoons brown sugar

¾ teaspoon ground cumin

½ teaspoon garlic powder

½ teaspoon salt

▲ **1 (1-pound) pork tenderloin, trimmed**

½ cup peach preserves

1 tablespoon apple-cider vinegar

1 teaspoon Dijon mustard

1 teaspoon minced chipotle en adobo

▲ **4 peaches, halved and pitted**

▲ Healthy Extra

Lightly spray asparagus spears and red bell pepper strips with nonstick spray and grill along with the pork.

1 Spray grill rack with nonstick spray. Preheat grill to medium-high or prepare medium-high fire.

2 Combine chili powder, 1 teaspoon of the brown sugar, the cumin, garlic powder, and ¼ teaspoon of the salt in small bowl. Rub mixture all over pork to coat. Stir together preserves, vinegar, mustard, chipotle, and remaining 1 teaspoon brown sugar and ¼ teaspoon salt in small bowl. Set aside.

3 Place pork on grill rack and grill, turning occasionally, 15 minutes. Brush pork with ¼ cup of the preserves mixture and grill, turning, until pork is glazed and browned and instant-read thermometer inserted into center of pork registers 160°F, 6–8 minutes longer. Transfer pork to cutting board and let stand 5 minutes.

4 Meanwhile, lightly spray peaches with nonstick spray. Place on grill rack and grill, brushing with remaining ¼ cup preserves mixture, until slightly softened, about 2 minutes on each side. Cut pork into 12 slices and serve with peaches.

PER SERVING (3 slices pork + 2 peach halves): 250 grams, 283 Cal, 4 g Total Fat, 1 g Sat Fat, 0 g Trans Fat, 62 mg Chol, 396 mg Sod, 40 g Carb, 26 g Sugar, 3 g Fib, 24 g Prot, 15 mg Calc.

Pork Chops with Carrot-Mint Slaw

SERVES 4

2 tablespoons minced lemongrass

1 tablespoon minced peeled fresh ginger

2 teaspoons reduced-sodium soy sauce

2 garlic cloves, minced

1 teaspoon brown sugar

1 teaspoon Asian (dark) sesame oil

▲ 4 (5-ounce) bone-in center-cut loin pork chops, trimmed

▲ 1 (10-ounce) bag shredded carrots

2 tablespoons chopped fresh mint

2 teaspoons lemon juice

1 teaspoon honey

1 Spray grill rack with nonstick spray. Preheat grill to medium-high or prepare medium-high fire.

2 Stir together lemongrass, ginger, soy sauce, garlic, brown sugar, and oil in small bowl. Brush both sides of chops with lemongrass mixture. Place chops on grill rack and grill, turning, until instant-read thermometer inserted into center of each chop registers 160°F, about 4 minutes on each side.

3 Meanwhile, to make slaw, toss together carrots, mint, lemon juice, and honey in large bowl until well mixed. Serve pork chops with slaw.

PER SERVING (1 pork chop + ³/₄ cup slaw): 230 grams, 185 Cal, 7 g Total Fat, 2 g Sat Fat, 0 g Trans Fat, 59 mg Chol, 178 mg Sod, 11 g Carb, 6 g Sugar, 2 g Fib, 20 g Prot, 48 mg Calc.

Grilled Lamb Koftas with Yogurt-Cilantro Sauce

Grilled Lamb Koftas with Yogurt-Cilantro Sauce

SERVES 4

1 pound ground lean lamb

▲ ½ small onion, shredded

3 tablespoons chopped fresh cilantro

1 tablespoon pine nuts, chopped

1 garlic clove, minced

1 teaspoon ground cumin

½ teaspoon ground allspice

½ teaspoon salt

4 (6-inch) whole wheat pocketless pita breads

▲ ½ cup plain fat-free Greek yogurt

1 tablespoon lemon juice

▲ 2 cups mixed baby greens

▲ Healthy Extra

Serve a salad alongside: Toss together 1 cup halved cherry tomatoes, 1 chopped small cucumber, and 1 chopped green bell pepper and sprinkle with red-wine vinegar, dried oregano, and salt and black pepper to taste.

1 Spray grill rack with nonstick spray. Preheat grill to medium-high or prepare medium-high fire. If using wooden skewers, soak 8 (8-inch) wooden skewers in water 15 minutes.

2 Meanwhile, mix together lamb, onion, 2 tablespoons of the cilantro, the pine nuts, garlic, cumin, allspice, and salt in large bowl until thoroughly combined. With damp hands, shape lamb mixture into 8 (1 x 4-inch) sausage shapes. Thread lamb koftas lengthwise onto skewers, then taper ends of each kofta. Place skewers on grill rack and grill, turning often, until lamb is evenly browned and cooked through, 8–10 minutes. Place pita breads on grill rack and grill until warmed, 1 minute on each side.

3 Meanwhile, to make sauce, stir together yogurt, lemon juice, and remaining 1 tablespoon cilantro in small bowl. Place pita breads on serving plates; top evenly with greens. Slide koftas off skewers onto greens (2 koftas on each pita). Drizzle evenly with sauce.

9 PointsPlus⊕ value ™ Per Serving

PER SERVING (1 plate): 200 grams, 359 Cal, 10 g Total Fat, 3 g Sat Fat, 0 g Trans Fat, 64 mg Chol, 710 mg Sod, 40 g Carb, 3 g Sugar, 6 g Fib, 30 g Prot, 51 mg Calc.

Smoky Lamb and Lentil Stew

12 ounces lean ground lamb

▲ 1 sweet onion, thinly sliced

2 garlic cloves, minced

▲ 3 cups reduced-sodium chicken broth

▲ 1 cup lentils, picked over and rinsed

▲ 1 medium zucchini, chopped

▲ 1 tomato, chopped

½ teaspoon smoked or regular paprika

½ teaspoon salt

1 tablespoon chopped fresh thyme

1 Combine lamb, onion, and garlic in large saucepan and set over medium heat. Cook, breaking lamb apart with wooden spoon until lamb is browned, about 5 minutes.

2 Add broth, lentils, zucchini, tomato, paprika, and salt to saucepan; bring to boil. Reduce heat and simmer until lentils are tender, about 20 minutes. Remove from heat; stir in thyme.

9 PointsPlus® value ™

Per Serving

PER SERVING (about 1 ¼ cups): 384 grams, 383 Cal, 13 g Total Fat, 6 g Sat Fat, 0 g Trans Fat, 62 mg Chol, 451 mg Sod, 34 g Total Carb, 6 g Total Sugar, 12 g Fib, 32 g Prot, 51 mg Calc.

▲ Healthy Extra

Add 2 cups chopped escarole or kale to the stew during the last 10 minutes of cooking.

Grilled Chicken with Tomato Chimichurri Sauce

SERVES 4

1 ½ cups lightly packed flat-leaf parsley leaves

6 anchovy fillets, drained and patted dry with paper towels

3 tablespoons capers, drained

3 tablespoons lime juice

4 teaspoons olive oil

1 tablespoon water

1 garlic clove, chopped

¼ teaspoon coarsely ground black pepper

▲ 4 (5-ounce) skinless boneless chicken breasts

▲ 1 plum tomato, chopped

1 Spray grill rack with nonstick spray. Preheat grill to medium-high or prepare medium-high fire.

2 Place parsley, anchovies, capers, lime juice, oil, water, garlic, and pepper in mini-food processor and pulse until pureed. Transfer ¼ cup of the mixture to shallow dish; add chicken and turn to coat. Let stand at room temperature 10 minutes.

3 To make sauce, place remaining parsley mixture in small bowl and stir in tomato. Set aside.

4 Remove chicken from marinade; discard marinade. Place chicken on grill rack and grill, turning often, until chicken is cooked through, 8–10 minutes. Serve with sauce.

PER SERVING *(1 chicken breast + about 2 tablespoons sauce): 195 grams, 223 Cal, 9 g Total Fat, 2 g Sat Fat, 0 g Trans Fat, 83 mg Chol, 494 mg Sod, 4 g Carb, 1 g Sugar, 1 g Fib, 31 g Prot, 67 mg Calc.*

F.Y.I.

If you're not a fan of anchovies, you can reduce the number used in this recipe to just two for a hint of flavor, or you can leave them out. If you do omit them, add ¼ teaspoon salt to the sauce.

Pecan-Crusted Chicken with Cilantro Slaw

SERVES 4

CHICKEN

▲ *1 large egg white*

¼ teaspoon salt

⅛ teaspoon cayenne

¾ cup whole wheat panko bread crumbs

¼ cup finely chopped pecans

▲ *4 (5-ounce) skinless boneless chicken breasts*

2 teaspoons olive oil

2 teaspoons unsalted butter

SLAW

3 tablespoons lime juice

¼ teaspoon salt

¼ teaspoon coarsely ground black pepper

▲ *4 cups shredded green and red cabbage*

½ cup chopped fresh cilantro

1 Preheat oven to 400°F.

2 To make chicken, whisk together egg white, salt, and cayenne in shallow dish. Mix together panko and pecans on sheet of wax paper.

3 Dip chicken in egg white mixture, then coat on all sides with panko mixture, pressing lightly so it adheres.

4 Heat oil and butter in large ovenproof nonstick skillet over medium-high heat. Add chicken and cook until bottom is browned, 4 minutes. Turn chicken and transfer skillet to oven. Bake until chicken is cooked through, about 10 minutes.

5 Meanwhile, to make slaw, stir together lime juice, salt, and pepper in medium bowl. Add cabbage and cilantro and toss to coat. Serve chicken with slaw.

PER SERVING *(1 chicken breast + ¾ cup slaw): 232 grams, 313 Cal, 13 g Total Fat, 3 g Sat Fat, 0 g Trans Fat, 83 mg Chol, 403 mg Sod, 16 g Carb, 1 g Sugar, 4 g Fib, 33 g Prot, 55 mg Calc.*

F.Y.I.

If your nonstick skillet doesn't have an ovenproof handle, **wrap the handle with a double-thickness of aluminum foil** to protect it from the heat.

*Pecan-Crusted Chicken
with Cilantro Slaw*

Brazilian Chicken with Black Beans and Rice

SERVES 4

▲ *¹/₂ cup instant brown rice*

¹/₂ teaspoon ground cumin

¹/₂ teaspoon ground coriander

¹/₂ teaspoon dried thyme

¹/₄ teaspoon salt

¹/₈ teaspoon ground allspice

▲ *4 (5-ounce) skinless boneless chicken breasts*

1 teaspoon olive oil

▲ *1 medium onion, chopped*

2 tablespoons water

1 garlic clove, minced

▲ *1 (15 ¹/₂-ounce) can black beans, rinsed and drained*

1 tablespoon lime juice

2 tablespoons chopped fresh cilantro

1 Cook rice according to package directions, omitting salt and butter.

2 Meanwhile, stir together cumin, coriander, thyme, salt, and allspice in medium bowl. Add chicken and toss to coat.

3 Heat oil in large nonstick skillet over medium-high heat. Add chicken and cook, turning occasionally, until cooked through, about 8 minutes. Transfer to plate; cover to keep warm.

4 Add onion and water to same skillet and cook over medium heat, stirring occasionally, until softened, 3 minutes. Add garlic and cook, stirring constantly, until fragrant, 30 seconds. Add beans and lime juice and cook, stirring often, until heated through, about 2 minutes. Stir in rice and 1 tablespoon of the cilantro.

5 Divide chicken and rice and beans evenly among 4 serving plates. Sprinkle evenly with remaining 1 tablespoon cilantro.

PER SERVING (*1 chicken breast + ³/₄ cup rice and beans): 217 grams, 280 Cal, 5 g Total Fat, 1 g Sat Fat, 0 g Trans Fat, 78 mg Chol, 443 mg Sod, 27 g Carb, 3 g Sugar, 7 g Fib, 34 g Prot, 64 mg Calc.*

▲ Healthy Extra

Serve this dish with a crispy vegetable salad. Toss together 1 peeled and chopped jicama, 1 chopped English (seedless) cucumber, 1 chopped red bell pepper, a squeeze of lime juice, and salt and cayenne to taste.

Crispy Chicken with Lemon-Basil Dip

SERVES 4

2 tablespoons reduced-fat mayonnaise

▲ **2 tablespoons plus ½ cup plain fat-free yogurt**

2 teaspoons Dijon mustard

¾ teaspoon salt

½ teaspoon black pepper

▲ **1 pound chicken tenders, each cut lengthwise in half**

¾ cup whole wheat panko bread crumbs

2 tablespoons chopped fresh basil

1 teaspoon grated lemon zest

1 garlic clove, minced

1 Place oven rack in top third of oven. Preheat oven to 400°F. Spray large baking sheet with nonstick spray.

2 Stir together mayonnaise, 2 tablespoons of the yogurt, the mustard, ½ teaspoon of the salt, and ¼ teaspoon of the pepper in medium bowl. Add chicken and toss to coat. Place panko on sheet of wax paper. Dip chicken pieces, one at a time, into panko, pressing gently to coat. Place on prepared baking sheet and lightly spray with nonstick spray. Bake 10 minutes.

3 Meanwhile, to make dip, stir together remaining ½ cup yogurt, the basil, lemon zest, garlic, and remaining ¼ teaspoon salt and ¼ teaspoon pepper in small bowl; set aside.

4 Remove baking sheet from oven; turn chicken over. Lightly spray with nonstick spray. Return to oven; bake until chicken is browned and cooked through, 10 minutes longer. Serve chicken with dip.

5 PointsPlus® value Per Serving

PER SERVING (4 pieces chicken + 2 tablespoons dip): 150 grams, 215 Cal, 4 g Total Fat, 1 g Sat Fat, 0 g Trans Fat, 63 mg Chol, 663 mg Sod, 15 g Carb, 4 g Sugar, 2 g Fib, 27 g Prot, 93 mg Calc.

Caribbean Chicken and Pineapple Kebabs

SERVES 4

▲ **1 bunch scallions**

   2 tablespoons Worcestershire sauce

   1 tablespoon water

   2 teaspoons canola oil

   ¾ teaspoon dried thyme

   ½ teaspoon ground allspice

   ¼ teaspoon red pepper flakes

   1 garlic clove, chopped

▲ **1 pound chicken tenders**

▲ **1 red bell pepper, cut into 1-inch pieces**

▲ **2 cups (1-inch) chunks fresh pineapple**

To add more colorful and nutritious vegetables to this dish, use one more skewer for each serving and add grape tomatoes, chunks of zucchini, and small whole mushrooms to the kebabs.

1 Spray grill rack with nonstick spray. Preheat grill to medium-high or prepare medium-high fire.

2 Cut white ends of scallions into 2-inch pieces and set aside. Chop green tops of scallions and place in blender with Worcestershire sauce, water, oil, thyme, allspice, pepper flakes, and garlic; blend until smooth, adding additional water 1 tablespoon at a time if necessary. Transfer to medium bowl; add chicken and toss to coat. Let stand at room temperature 10 minutes.

3 Thread chicken, reserved scallions, bell pepper, and pineapple onto 8 (8-inch) metal skewers. Place skewers on grill rack and grill, turning often, until chicken is cooked through, 8–10 minutes.

PER SERVING (2 skewers): 173 grams, 206 Cal, 5 g Total Fat, 1 g Sat Fat, 0 g Trans Fat, 63 mg Chol, 152 mg Sod, 15 g Carb, 10 g Sugar, 3 g Fib, 24 g Prot, 51 mg Calc.

Pressure Cooker Moroccan Chicken Stew

SERVES 4

2 teaspoons olive oil

4 (6-ounce) skinless bone-in chicken thighs

▲ **1 medium onion, chopped**

2 garlic cloves, minced

1 1/2 teaspoons ground coriander

1 1/2 teaspoons ground cumin

1 teaspoon grated peeled fresh ginger

1/2 teaspoon salt

1/4 teaspoon cayenne

▲ **3 (8-ounce) sweet potatoes, peeled and cut into 2-inch chunks**

▲ **1 cup reduced-sodium chicken broth**

▲ **1 (15 1/2-ounce) can chickpeas, rinsed and drained**

1/2 cup raisins

▲ **1 (5-ounce) package baby spinach**

1 Heat oil in 6-quart pressure cooker over medium-high heat. Add chicken and cook until browned, about 2 minutes on each side. Transfer to plate. Add onion and cook, stirring occasionally, until softened, 3 minutes. Add garlic, coriander, cumin, ginger, salt, and cayenne and cook, stirring constantly, until fragrant, 30 seconds. Return chicken to pressure cooker; add potatoes and broth.

2 Lock lid in place and increase heat to high. Bring cooker to high pressure, following manufacturer's directions. Reduce heat and cook at high pressure 9 minutes.

3 Place pot in sink and run cold water over lid to bring pressure down quickly. When pressure indicator releases, remove pot from sink and unlock lid, following manufacturer's directions.

4 Set pressure cooker over medium-high heat. Add chickpeas and raisins and cook, stirring often, until heated through, about 2 minutes. Add spinach, and cook, stirring constantly, just until spinach wilts, 1 minute longer.

PER SERVING *(1 chicken thigh + 1 cup chickpea mixture): 410 grams, 513 Cal, 13 g Total Fat, 3 g Sat Fat, 0 g Trans Fat, 86 mg Chol, 636 mg Sod, 64 g Carb, 24 g Sugar, 11 g Fib, 34 g Prot, 152 mg Calc.*

Chicken-Apple Burgers with Caper Mayonnaise

SERVES 4

BURGERS

▲ **1 pound ground skinless chicken breast**

▲ **$1/2$ cup shredded peeled Granny Smith apple**

$1/2$ cup fresh whole wheat bread crumbs

▲ **$1/4$ cup finely chopped celery**

▲ **1 scallion, finely chopped**

$1/2$ teaspoon salt

$1/4$ teaspoon coarsely ground black pepper

MAYONNAISE

$1/4$ cup fat-free mayonnaise

1 teaspoon minced fresh tarragon

1 teaspoon capers, drained and minced

$1/2$ teaspoon lemon juice

$1/8$ teaspoon coarsely ground black pepper

▲ **4 thick slices beefsteak tomato**

▲ **4 large Boston lettuce leaves**

1 To make burgers, combine all burger ingredients in medium bowl. With damp hands, shape mixture into 4 ($1/2$-inch-thick) patties.

2 Spray large ridged grill pan or skillet with nonstick spray and set over medium-high heat. Add patties and cook until instant-read thermometer inserted into side of each burger registers 165°F, 6–7 minutes on each side.

3 Meanwhile, to make mayonnaise, stir together all mayonnaise ingredients in small bowl.

4 Divide tomato slices and lettuce leaves among 4 serving plates. Top each with 1 burger. Spoon mayonnaise evenly over burgers.

PER SERVING (1 plate): 202 grams, 204 Cal, 4 g Total Fat, 1 g Sat Fat, 0 g Trans Fat, 64 mg Chol, 644 mg Sod, 14 g Carb, 6 g Sugar, 2 g Fib, 25 g Prot, 61 mg Calc.

▲Healthy Extra

For an additional **3 PointsPlus** value, serve each burger in a split and toasted light English muffin.

Grilled Turkey Cutlets with Watermelon Salsa

SERVES 4

SALSA

▲ **2 cups diced seedless watermelon**

2 tablespoons chopped fresh cilantro

▲ **2 tablespoons diced red onion**

2 tablespoons lime juice

▲ **1 jalapeño pepper, seeded and minced**

TURKEY

1 garlic clove, minced

1 teaspoon olive oil

¹⁄₂ teaspoon dried oregano

¹⁄₂ teaspoon chili powder

¹⁄₂ teaspoon ground cumin

¹⁄₄ teaspoon salt

▲ **4 (¹⁄₄-pound) turkey breast cutlets**

1 Spray grill rack with nonstick spray. Preheat grill to medium or prepare medium fire.

2 To make salsa, stir together all salsa ingredients in medium bowl. Set aside.

3 To make turkey, stir together garlic, oil, oregano, chili powder, cumin, and salt in small bowl. Rub garlic mixture over both sides of turkey.

4 Place turkey on grill rack and grill, turning often, until turkey is cooked through, 5–7 minutes. Serve turkey with salsa.

4 PointsPlus® value™ Per Serving

PER SERVING (1 turkey cutlet + ³⁄₄ cup salsa): 206 grams, 163 Cal, 2 g Total Fat, 0 g Sat Fat, 0 g Trans Fat, 45 mg Chol, 250 mg Sod, 8 g Carb, 5 g Sugar, 1 g Fib, 29 g Prot, 14 mg Calc.

F.Y.I.

You can also serve this salsa with grilled chicken breasts, salmon fillets, scallops, or shrimp. Fresh mint or basil is a delicious alternative to the cilantro.

Grilled Turkey
Saltimbocca

Grilled Turkey Saltimbocca

SERVES 4

- ▲ **4 (¼-pound) turkey breast cutlets**
- **4 tablespoons soft goat cheese**
- **¼ teaspoon coarsely ground black pepper**
- ▲ **¾ pound thin asparagus (about 32 spears), trimmed**
- **12 fresh sage leaves**
- **8 slices prosciutto (about 2 ounces)**

F.Y.I.

If you don't want to light up the grill, **cook the turkey rolls** in a large nonstick grill pan or skillet, covered, turning occasionally, until the turkey is cooked through, 10–12 minutes.

1 Spray grill rack with nonstick spray. Preheat grill to medium or prepare medium fire. If using wooden skewers to secure rolls, soak 4 small wooden skewers in water 15 minutes.

2 Place turkey cutlets in single layer between 2 sheets of plastic wrap. With meat mallet or rolling pin, lightly pound to ⅛-inch thickness. Spread 1 tablespoon of the goat cheese on each cutlet; sprinkle evenly with pepper. Place 8 asparagus spears crosswise on each cutlet. Roll up cutlets beginning with short side. Place 3 sage leaves on each roll, then wrap each roll with 2 slices prosciutto. Secure each roll with skewer.

3 Place rolls on grill rack and grill, covered, turning occasionally, until turkey is cooked through, 12–15 minutes.

4 Transfer rolls to cutting board; remove skewers. Serve at once.

PER SERVING *(1 roll): 158 grams, 188 Cal, 4 g Total Fat, 2 g Sat Fat, 0 g Trans Fat, 59 mg Chol, 508 mg Sod, 4 g Carb, 2 g Sugar, 2 g Fib, 35 g Prot, 31 mg Calc.*

Duck Breasts with Balsamic Cranberries

SERVES 4

4 (5-ounce) skinless boneless duck breasts

¼ teaspoon salt

⅛ teaspoon coarsely ground black pepper

2 teaspoons olive oil

1 large shallot, thinly sliced

1 garlic clove, minced

½ cup ruby port wine

▲ ½ cup reduced-sodium chicken broth

⅓ cup dried cranberries

2 tablespoons balsamic vinegar

1 Sprinkle duck with salt and pepper. Heat 1 teaspoon of the oil in large nonstick skillet over medium-high heat. Add duck and cook 3–4 minutes on each side for medium-rare. Transfer to cutting board; cover to keep warm.

2 To make sauce, heat remaining 1 teaspoon oil in same skillet over medium-high heat. Add shallot and cook, stirring often, until lightly browned, 2–3 minutes. Add garlic and cook, stirring constantly, until fragrant, 30 seconds. Add port, broth, cranberries, vinegar, and any accumulated juices on cutting board with duck; bring to boil. Boil, stirring occasionally, until sauce is reduced to ¾ cup, about 5 minutes. Cut duck crosswise into ¼-inch-thick slices and serve with sauce.

▲ **Healthy Extra**

Make an accompanying salad: Toss together 6 cups mixed baby greens, 1 thinly sliced Belgian endive, 1 cup sliced fresh mushrooms, a splash of seasoned rice vinegar, and salt and black pepper to taste.

PER SERVING (1 duck breast + 3 tablespoons sauce): 258 grams, 288 Cal, 8 g Total Fat, 2 g Sat Fat, 0 g Trans Fat, 109 mg Chol, 301 mg Sod, 15 g Carb, 10 g Sugar, 1 g Fib, 29 g Prot, 16 mg Calc.

Tuna and Penne Salad with Basil and Olives

SERVES 4

▲ **2 cups (about 6 ounces) whole wheat penne**

▲ **½ pound slender green beans or haricots verts, trimmed**

▲ **2 celery stalks, thinly sliced**

▲ **1 red bell pepper, cut into ¾-inch chunks**

▲ **1 (6-ounce) can water-packed light tuna, drained and flaked**

½ cup chopped fresh basil

8 oil-cured black olives, pitted and finely chopped

1 tablespoon capers, drained

Juice of 1 lemon

2 teaspoons extra-virgin olive oil

¼ teaspoon black pepper

1 Cook penne according to package directions, omitting salt if desired and adding beans during last 3 minutes of cooking. Drain and rinse under cold running water; drain again.

2 Meanwhile, stir together celery, bell pepper, tuna, basil, olives, capers, lemon juice, oil, and black pepper in large bowl. Add pasta mixture to celery mixture and toss to combine.

 PER SERVING (2 cups): 210 grams, 273 Cal, 7 g Total Fat, 1 g Sat Fat, 0 g Trans Fat, 23 mg Chol, 370 mg Sod, 36 g Carb, 5 g Sugar, 9 g Fib, 18 g Prot, 67 mg Calc.

Add 1 chopped large tomato and 2 chopped Kirby cucumbers to the salad.

Salmon with Coconut-Tomato Sauce

SERVES 4

2 teaspoons canola oil

▲ 1 small onion, finely chopped

1 tablespoon minced peeled fresh ginger

1 garlic clove, minced

▲ ½ cup drained canned petite diced tomatoes

½ cup light (reduced-fat) coconut milk

Pinch cayenne

▲ 12 cherry tomatoes, halved

1 pound skinless salmon fillets, cut into 1-inch pieces

½ teaspoon salt

2 teaspoons lime juice

3 tablespoons chopped fresh cilantro

1 Heat oil in large nonstick skillet over medium-high heat. Add onion and cook, stirring often, until softened, about 5 minutes. Add ginger and garlic and cook, stirring constantly, until fragrant, 30 seconds. Add diced tomatoes, coconut milk, and cayenne; bring to simmer and cook, covered, 5 minutes.

2 Add cherry tomatoes to skillet and simmer just until tomatoes begin to soften, 1–2 minutes. Sprinkle salmon with salt. Add salmon and lime juice to skillet and cook, stirring gently, until salmon is just opaque in center, 3–4 minutes. Stir in cilantro.

PER SERVING *(1 cup): 258 grams, 250 Cal, 13 g Total Fat, 1 g Sat Fat, 0 g Trans Fat, 72 mg Chol, 423 mg Sod, 7 g Carb, 3 g Sugar, 1 g Fib, 27 g Prot, 31 mg Calc.*

▲ *Healthy Extra*

To soak up the creamy coconut sauce, serve the salmon with brown rice (⅔ cup cooked brown rice per serving will increase the **PointsPlus** value by **3**).

Salmon with
Coconut-Tomato Sauce

Potato-Crusted Cod with Horseradish Sauce

SERVES 4

½ **cup low-fat mayonnaise**

2 tablespoons Dijon mustard

1 tablespoon prepared horseradish, drained

1 tablespoon minced fresh chives

▲ **4 (5-ounce) cod fillets**

1 cup refrigerated shredded potatoes

¼ **teaspoon salt**

½ **teaspoon black pepper**

2 teaspoons canola oil

F.Y.I.

When cooking the fillets, don't be tempted to move them until the potatoes have set and started to brown. Otherwise, the potato topping may separate from the fish.

1 Preheat oven to 400°F. Spray medium baking sheet with nonstick spray.

2 Stir together mayonnaise, mustard, horseradish, and chives in small bowl. Transfer half of mayonnaise mixture to another small bowl and refrigerate, covered, until ready to serve.

3 Spread remaining mayonnaise mixture evenly on top of fillets. Top each fillet with ¼ cup of the potatoes, pressing to form even layer. Sprinkle potatoes with salt and pepper.

4 Heat 1 teaspoon of the oil in large nonstick skillet over medium-high heat. Carefully place 2 fillets, potato side down, in skillet and cook, without moving, until potatoes are set and browned, 6–8 minutes. If potatoes begin to brown too quickly, reduce heat. Transfer fillets, crust side up, to prepared baking sheet. Repeat with remaining oil and fillets. Bake, without turning, until fish is just opaque in center, 8–10 minutes. Serve with reserved mayonnaise mixture.

PER SERVING *(1 fish fillet + 1 tablespoon sauce): 210 grams, 215 Cal, 8 g Total Fat, 1 g Sat Fat, 0 g Trans Fat, 54 mg Chol, 693 mg Sod, 13 g Carb, 2 g Sugar, 1 g Fib, 23 g Prot, 25 mg Calc.*

Thai Shrimp Summer Rolls

▲ **4 ounces brown rice stick noodles**

¼ cup reduced-sodium soy sauce

Juice of 1 lime

2 teaspoons sugar

1 teaspoon chili-garlic sauce

8 (6-inch) round rice paper wrappers

▲ **4 large Boston lettuce leaves, each cut lengthwise in half**

▲ **1 English (seedless) cucumber, cut into julienne strips**

▲ **1 (8-ounce) bag shredded carrots (about 2 cups)**

▲ **24 cooked peeled and deveined medium shrimp, each cut lengthwise in half**

8 sprigs fresh mint

1 Place noodles in large bowl. Add boiling water to cover. Let stand until softened, about 10 minutes. Drain, rinse with cold water, and drain again. Coarsely chop noodles.

2 Meanwhile, to make dipping sauce, whisk together soy sauce, lime juice, sugar, and chili-garlic sauce in small bowl.

3 To assemble rolls, working one at a time, dip rice wrapper in bowl of warm water; let stand just until soft, about 30 seconds. Place on clean kitchen towel. Place 1 lettuce leaf half in center of each wrapper. Top lettuce with one-eighth of the noodles, cucumber, and carrots. Then top with 6 shrimp halves and 1 mint sprig. Fold in sides, then roll up to completely enclose filling. Gently press to seal. Cut each roll diagonally in half. Serve with dipping sauce.

PER SERVING *(2 rolls + generous 1 tablespoon sauce): 215 grams, 255 Cal, 2 g Total Fat, 0 g Sat Fat, 0 g Trans Fat, 55 mg Chol, 718 mg Sod, 44 g Carb, 7 g Sugar, 4 g Fib, 16 g Prot, 61 mg Calc.*

F.Y.I.

As you assemble the rolls, place them on a platter and cover with damp paper towels **to prevent them from drying out**.

Steamed Striped Bass with Sake-Ginger Broth

Steamed Striped Bass with Sake-Ginger Broth

SERVES 4

- ▲ *¾ cup reduced-sodium chicken broth*
- *¼ cup sake*
- *¼ cup mirin*
- *2 tablespoons reduced-sodium soy sauce*
- *1 tablespoon minced peeled fresh ginger*
- *2 garlic cloves, thinly sliced*
- *2 teaspoons Asian (dark) sesame oil*
- *1 small whole dried chile pepper*
- ▲ *¾ pound shiitake mushrooms, tough stems removed*
- ▲ *½ cup thinly sliced scallions*
- ▲ *6 large Boston lettuce leaves*
- ▲ *4 (5-ounce) striped bass fillets*
- ▲ *¼ cup diced red bell pepper*

1 To make broth, combine chicken broth, sake, mirin, soy sauce, ginger, garlic, oil, and chile pepper in large deep skillet; bring to boil. Add mushrooms and ¼ cup of the scallions; return to boil. Reduce heat and simmer, stirring occasionally, until mushrooms are tender, 4–5 minutes.

2 Meanwhile, arrange lettuce leaves in bottom of large steamer basket; arrange fish fillets on top of lettuce. Sprinkle fish with bell pepper and remaining ¼ cup scallions. Set steamer basket in large skillet over 1 inch of boiling water. Cover tightly and steam just until fish is opaque in center, 6–8 minutes.

3 Transfer lettuce leaves and fish to 4 shallow serving bowls; spoon broth mixture evenly over fish.

5 PointsPlus© value

Per Serving

PER SERVING *(1 fish fillet + about ⅓ cup broth mixture): 188 grams, 256 Cal, 6 g Total Fat, 1 g Sat Fat, 0 g Trans Fat, 117 mg Chol, 477 mg Sod, 14 g Carb, 6 g Sugar, 2 g Fib, 28 g Prot, 49 mg Calc.*

Prosciutto-Wrapped Scallop Salad

¼ *cup orange juice*

1 tablespoon seasoned rice vinegar

1 small shallot, minced

2 teaspoons olive oil

¼ *teaspoon coarsely ground pepper*

Pinch salt

▲ *2 navel oranges, peeled and cut into sections*

▲ *1 small fennel bulb, thinly sliced*

▲ *1 Granny Smith apple, peeled, cored, and thinly sliced*

¼ *cup fresh cilantro leaves*

▲ *12 large sea scallops*

2 ounces prosciutto, cut into 12 (1-inch-wide) strips

1 Whisk together orange juice, vinegar, shallot, 1 teaspoon of the oil, ⅛ teaspoon of the pepper, and the salt in large bowl. Add orange sections, fennel, apple, and cilantro; toss gently to coat. Let stand, stirring once, 10 minutes.

2 Meanwhile, pat scallops dry with paper towels. Wrap 1 strip prosciutto around each scallop. Sprinkle with the remaining ⅛ teaspoon pepper.

3 Heat remaining 1 teaspoon oil in large nonstick skillet over medium-high heat. Add scallops and cook until scallops are just opaque in center and prosciutto is browned, 2–3 minutes on each side. Serve scallops with salad.

PER SERVING *(3 scallops + ½ cup salad):*
194 grams, 194 Cal, 5 g Total Fat, 1 g Sat Fat,
0 g Trans Fat, 44 mg Chol, 647 mg Sod, 22 g Carb,
12 g Sugar, 2 g Fib, 19 g Prot, 56 mg Calc.

Prosciutto-Wrapped Scallop Salad

Pressure Cooker Winter Vegetable and Bean Soup

SERVES 4

2 teaspoons olive oil

▲ 1 medium onion, chopped

2 garlic cloves, minced

1 teaspoon curry powder

½ teaspoon salt

½ teaspoon grated peeled fresh ginger

⅛ teaspoon cayenne

▲ 2 cups reduced-sodium vegetable broth

2 cups water

▲ 3 carrots, chopped

▲ 2 medium (8-ounce) baking potatoes, peeled and chopped

▲ 2 medium (8-ounce) turnips, peeled and chopped

▲ 1 (1 ¾-pound) butternut squash, peeled, seeded, and chopped

▲ 1 (15-ounce) can cannellini (white kidney) beans, rinsed and drained

1 Heat oil in 6-quart pressure cooker over medium-high heat. Add onion and cook, stirring occasionally, until softened, 3 minutes. Add garlic, curry powder, salt, ginger, and cayenne and cook, stirring constantly, until fragrant, 30 seconds. Add broth, water, carrots, potatoes, turnips, and squash.

2 Lock lid in place and increase heat to high. Bring cooker to high pressure, following manufacturer's directions. Reduce heat and cook at high pressure 8 minutes.

3 Place pot in sink and run cold water over lid to bring pressure down quickly. When pressure indicator releases, remove pot from sink and unlock lid, following manufacturer's directions.

4 Set pressure cooker over medium-high heat; add beans and cook until heated through, about 2 minutes.

PER SERVING (2 cups): 598 grams, 320 Cal, 4 g Total Fat, 0 g Sat Fat, 0 g Trans Fat, 0 mg Chol, 509 mg Sod, 67 g Carb, 16 g Sugar, 16 g Fib, 10 g Prot, 191 mg Calc.

F.Y.I.

To save time, look for peeled, seeded, and cut-up butternut squash in the produce section of large supermarkets. For this recipe, buy about 1 pound of prepared squash.

The ultimate Grocery List

If a weekly trip to the grocery store is your routine, then make the most efficient use of the time you spend shopping with these prepping pointers:

■ **Try New Foods.** Jot down a list of key ingredients that make up the meals your family eats on a weekly basis, then think about how to boost variety. For example, if you regularly eat cereal for breakfast, consider oatmeal for a few mornings; if baked chicken is a dinner staple, try pork cutlets, and so on. Aim to introduce at least one new lean protein, whole grain, fruit, and vegetable each week.

■ **Write It Down.** Keep a notepad and pen on your refrigerator so you can jot down any perishables or pantry staples that need replenishing. Or go high tech (see page 87).

■ **Stock Up on Staples.** Do a pantry check every two weeks. Must-have staples to keep on hand include whole grains (such as brown rice, whole wheat pasta, oats, and barley), canned beans, and canned tomato products. Again, try to include a new pantry staple—including condiments—every two weeks. Look through the Weight Watchers Power Foods list to get ideas for new healthy foods you might like to try.

■ **Clip Coupons Wisely.** Do a coupon/circular check, comparing your list to clipped coupons you've gathered, as well as what's on sale at your local market. Don't let a coupon or a sale entice you into buying foods you wouldn't ordinarily buy. Highly processed, high calorie foods are not a bargain at any price. Sometimes store-brand versions of items such as grains, beans, and canned tomato products are a better deal than using a coupon for a brand name product.

■ **Map It Out.** Write or type your final list in the order of your market's layout so you can move smoothly from one side of the supermarket to the other.

Lemon-Basil Tofu with Pasta and Zucchini

Lemon-Basil Tofu with Pasta and Zucchini

SERVES 4

▲ **6 ounces whole wheat spaghetti**

▲ **1 medium zucchini, cut into julienne strips**

2 teaspoons olive oil

▲ **1 (14-ounce) package extra-firm tofu, drained, patted dry, and cut into 1-inch cubes**

3 garlic cloves, minced

1/4 teaspoon red pepper flakes

▲ **1/3 cup reduced-sodium vegetable broth**

1/4 cup lemon juice

1/2 teaspoon salt

▲ **1 cup cherry tomatoes, quartered**

2 tablespoons thinly sliced fresh basil

1 teaspoon unsalted butter

1 Cook spaghetti according to package directions, adding zucchini during last 1 minute of cooking. Drain and keep warm.

2 Meanwhile, heat 1 teaspoon of the oil in large nonstick skillet over medium-high heat. Add tofu and cook, turning often, until lightly browned on all sides, about 5 minutes. Transfer tofu to plate.

3 Heat remaining 1 teaspoon oil over medium-high heat in same skillet. Add garlic and pepper flakes and cook, stirring constantly, until fragrant, 30 seconds. Add broth, lemon juice, and salt and bring to boil. Boil until slightly thickened, about 2 minutes. Add tofu and tomatoes and cook, stirring often, just until tomatoes are heated through, 1 minute. Remove from heat and stir in basil and butter.

4 Divide pasta mixture evenly among 4 serving plates; top evenly with tofu mixture.

7 PointsPlus® value
Per Serving

PER SERVING *(1 cup pasta mixture + 3/4 cup tofu mixture): 286 grams, 288 Cal, 9 g Total Fat, 1 g Sat Fat, 0 g Trans Fat, 3 mg Chol, 314 mg Sod, 40 g Carb, 4 g Sugar, 8 g Fib, 16 g Prot, 226 mg Calc.*

▲ *Healthy Extra*

Stir in 2 cups of baby spinach when you add the basil in step 3.

Sesame Grilled Portobellos with Sriracha Mayonnaise

SERVES 4

⅓ cup fat-free mayonnaise

1 ½ teaspoons grated peeled fresh ginger

1 teaspoon Sriracha (Asian hot chile sauce)

3 tablespoons chopped fresh mint

2 tablespoons reduced-sodium soy sauce

2 teaspoons canola oil

1 teaspoon Asian (dark) sesame oil

▲ *1 large red onion*

▲ *4 large portobello mushroom caps*

▲ *4 thick slices beefsteak tomato*

F.Y.I.

Huy Fong Foods brand **Sriracha was created** by a Vietnamese immigrant in California in the 1980s who couldn't find a hot sauce to his liking in the U.S. It has become an essential ingredient for restaurant chefs as well as home cooks.

1 Spray grill rack with nonstick spray. Preheat grill to medium or prepare medium fire.

2 Stir together mayonnaise, ginger, Sriracha, and 1 tablespoon of the mint in small bowl.

3 Stir together soy sauce, canola oil, and sesame oil in another small bowl. Cut 4 (½-inch-thick) slices from center of onion; reserve remaining onion for another use.

4 Place onion slices and mushrooms, rounded side down, on grill rack. Brush with half of the soy sauce mixture; grill 6 minutes. Turn mushrooms and onion slices; brush with remaining soy sauce mixture and grill until tender, 6–7 minutes longer.

5 Place mushrooms, rounded side down, on 4 serving plates. Top each mushroom with tomato slice and onion slice; top evenly with mayonnaise mixture. Sprinkle evenly with remaining 2 tablespoons mint.

PER SERVING (*1 stuffed mushroom + generous 1 tablespoon sauce*): *214 grams, 106 Cal, 5 g Total Fat, 1 g Sat Fat, 0 g Trans Fat, 2 mg Chol, 476 mg Sod, 15 g Carb, 6 g Sugar, 3 g Fib, 3 g Prot, 26 mg Calc.*

Mushroom and Arugula Omelette Roll

SERVES 2

2 teaspoons butter

▲ 1 (4-ounce) package sliced mixed wild mushrooms

1/4 teaspoon salt

▲ 4 large egg whites

▲ 2 large eggs

2 teaspoons mixed finely chopped fresh herbs (such as chives, thyme, and parsley)

1/8 teaspoon black pepper

▲ 1/2 cup lightly packed baby arugula

1 Melt 1 teaspoon of the butter in 12-inch nonstick skillet over medium-high heat. Add mushrooms and 1/8 teaspoon of the salt and cook, stirring often, until tender and lightly browned, about 5 minutes. Transfer mushrooms to plate.

2 Meanwhile, whisk together egg whites, eggs, 1 teaspoon of the mixed herbs, the pepper, and remaining 1/8 teaspoon salt in medium bowl.

3 Melt remaining 1 teaspoon butter over medium heat in same skillet. Pour egg mixture into skillet and cook until underside starts to set, about 30 seconds. Gently stir with heatproof spatula and cook, stirring occasionally to allow uncooked egg to run underneath, until eggs are set, about 3 minutes.

4 Slide omelette onto sheet of wax paper; arrange mushrooms and arugula on half of omelette. Starting from vegetable-topped side, roll omelette up jelly-roll style, using wax paper to lift omelette. Cut omelette diagonally into 4 slices. Divide slices evenly among 2 serving plates; sprinkle evenly with remaining 1 teaspoon mixed herbs.

4 PointsPlus value Per Serving

PER SERVING (1/2 omelette): 145 grams, 153 Cal, 9 g Total Fat, 4 g Sat Fat, 0 g Trans Fat, 225 mg Chol, 497 mg Sod, 4 g Carb, 2 g Sugar, 1 g Fib, 15 g Prot, 47 mg Calc.

Polenta Pizza
Margherita

Polenta Pizza Margherita

SERVES 4

▲ **1 (16-ounce) tube refrigerated fat-free plain polenta, cut into ¼-inch-thick slices**

¾ cup part-skim ricotta cheese

¼ cup grated Parmesan cheese

4 tablespoons thinly sliced fresh basil

¼ teaspoon red pepper flakes

▲ **2 plum tomatoes, thinly sliced and patted dry on paper towels**

½ cup shredded part-skim mozzarella cheese

1 Preheat broiler. Spray 10-inch pizza pan or large baking sheet with nonstick spray.

2 Place 1 slice of polenta in center of prepared pan; arrange remaining slices in 2 concentric circles around first slice, overlapping slightly to form 10-inch round. Lightly spray polenta with nonstick spray.

3 Broil polenta 4 inches from heat until lightly browned and heated through, 6–8 minutes.

4 Meanwhile, stir together ricotta, Parmesan, 3 tablespoons of the basil, and the pepper flakes.

5 Arrange tomato slices on polenta. Top tomatoes with dollops of ricotta mixture; sprinkle with mozzarella. Broil until tomatoes are hot and mozzarella is melted, about 4 minutes. Sprinkle with remaining 1 tablespoon basil. Cut into 4 wedges and serve at once.

PER SERVING *(1 wedge): 204 grams, 241 Cal, 8 g Total Fat, 5 g Sat Fat, 0 g Trans Fat, 26 mg Chol, 676 mg Sod, 27 g Carb, 3 g Sugar, 2 g Fib, 14 g Prot, 473 mg Calc.*

faster

In a hurry? If you've got just 20 minutes, you can make a satisfying spur-of-the moment weeknight dinner with these shortcut recipes that are packed with flavor. Not only are they doable—they're delicious!

20 MIN

PointsPlus®

PointsPlus®

Sirloin with Cherry Tomatoes and Basil

2 teaspoons olive oil

▲ 1 pound boneless sirloin steak, trimmed and cut into 4 equal pieces

¾ teaspoon salt

¼ teaspoon black pepper

1 garlic clove, minced

▲ 1 pint cherry or grape tomatoes, halved

1 tablespoon chopped fresh basil

1 Heat 1 teaspoon of the oil in large nonstick skillet over medium-high heat. Sprinkle steaks with ½ teaspoon of the salt and the pepper. Place in skillet and cook until instant-read thermometer inserted into side of each steak registers 145°F for medium, 3–4 minutes on each side. Transfer to platter and keep warm.

2 Heat remaining 1 teaspoon oil in same skillet over medium heat; add garlic and cook, stirring often, until softened, about 1 minute. Add tomatoes and remaining ¼ teaspoon salt and cook, stirring often, until heated through. Remove from heat and stir in basil. Spoon tomato mixture over steaks.

PER SERVING *(1 steak + about ½ cup tomato mixture): 185 grams, 191 Cal, 7 g Total Fat, 2 g Sat Fat, 0 g Trans Fat, 49 mg Chol, 494 mg Sod, 3 g Carb, 2 g Sugar, 1 g Fib, 27 g Prot, 28 mg Calc.*

F.Y.I.

In the summertime, **a combination of colorful chopped heirloom tomatoes** is a good substitute for the cherry tomatoes. You'll need 2 cups for this recipe.

Grilled Beef Fattoush Salad

SERVES ~~4~~ 6

4 tablespoons lemon juice

2 ½ teaspoons dried oregano

¾ teaspoon salt

½ teaspoon black pepper

▲ 1 (1 ¼-pound) flank steak, trimmed

2 tablespoons water

1 tablespoon extra-virgin olive oil

▲ 4 plum tomatoes, chopped

▲ 2 cups packed sliced romaine lettuce

▲ ½ English (seedless) cucumber, halved lengthwise and thinly sliced

2 (6-inch) whole wheat pita breads, toasted and cut into 8 wedges each

1 Spray broiler rack with olive oil nonstick spray; preheat broiler.

2 Whisk together 2 tablespoons of the lemon juice, 2 teaspoons of the oregano, ½ teaspoon of the salt, and ¼ of the teaspoon pepper in shallow baking dish. Add steak and turn to coat.

3 Place steak on prepared broiler rack and broil about 5 inches from heat until instant-read thermometer inserted into center of steak registers 145°F for medium, 5–6 minutes on each side. Transfer to cutting board and let stand 5 minutes.

4 Meanwhile, whisk together water, oil, and remaining 2 tablespoons lemon juice, ½ teaspoon oregano, ¼ teaspoon salt, and ¼ teaspoon pepper in large serving bowl. Add tomatoes, lettuce, and cucumber and toss to coat. Slice steak across grain into ~~12~~ 18 slices. Add sliced steak and pita wedges to bowl and toss again.

PER SERVING (3 slices steak and about 1 ⅔ cups salad): 207 grams, 226 Cal, 8 g Total Fat, 3 g Sat Fat, 0 g Trans Fat, 35 mg Chol, 448 mg Sod, 16 g Carb, 2 g Sugar, 3 g Fib, 23 g Prot, 39 mg Calc.

▲ *Healthy Extra*

Stir ⅓ cup sliced radishes in with the tomatoes, lettuce, and cucumber to add peppery crunch.

Weeknight Beef and Vegetable Stew

2 teaspoons canola oil

▲ 1 pound filet mignon, trimmed and cut into 1-inch chunks

1/2 teaspoon salt

1/4 teaspoon black pepper

▲ 2 celery stalks, thinly sliced

▲ 2 carrots, thinly sliced

▲ 1 onion, finely chopped

1 tablespoon water

1 tablespoon plus 1 teaspoon all-purpose flour

▲ 1 3/4 cups reduced-sodium beef broth

▲ 1 teaspoon tomato paste

1/2 teaspoon dried thyme

1 Heat 1 teaspoon of the oil in nonstick Dutch oven over medium-high heat. Sprinkle beef with salt and pepper. Place in Dutch oven and cook, stirring often, until browned, about 2 minutes. Transfer to plate.

2 Heat remaining 1 teaspoon oil in same Dutch oven over medium-high heat. Add celery, carrots, onion, and water. Reduce heat to medium and cook, covered, stirring occasionally, until vegetables soften, about 5 minutes.

3 Add flour to Dutch oven and stir until vegetables are coated. Add broth, tomato paste, and thyme. Bring to boil. Reduce heat and simmer, partially covered, until vegetables are almost tender, about 5 minutes. Return beef and any accumulated juices to Dutch oven and cook until beef is heated through and vegetables are tender, about 3 minutes.

6 PointsPlus value

Per Serving

PER SERVING (1 1/2 cups): 189 grams, 240 Cal, 10 g Total Fat, 3 g Sat Fat, 0 g Trans Fat, 67 mg Chol, 435 mg Sod, 10 g Carb, 5 g Sugar, 2 g Fib, 27 g Prot, 52 mg Calc.

F.Y.I.

To complete the meal, serve the stew with high fiber rolls (one 2-ounce roll per serving will increase the **PointsPlus** value by **4**.)

Weeknight Beef and Vegetable Stew

Beef Stroganoff Stir-Fry

▲ **6 ounces whole wheat noodles**

2 teaspoons canola oil

▲ **¾ pound boneless sirloin steak, trimmed and thinly sliced**

½ teaspoon salt

▲ **1 (10-ounce) package sliced cremini mushrooms**

2 tablespoons minced shallot

▲ **1 cup reduced-sodium beef broth**

2 teaspoons cornstarch

▲ **¼ cup fat-free sour cream**

¼ teaspoon black pepper

F.Y.I.

If you have the time, **partially freezing the steak** first makes cutting it into thin slices much easier. For extra flavor, sprinkle each serving of stir-fry with chopped fresh chives or minced scallion.

1 Cook noodles according to package directions, omitting salt if desired. Drain and keep warm.

2 Meanwhile, heat 1 teaspoon of the oil in large nonstick skillet over medium-high heat. Sprinkle steak with ¼ teaspoon of the salt. Place in skillet and stir-fry until browned, about 3 minutes. Transfer to plate.

3 Heat remaining 1 teaspoon oil in same skillet over medium-high heat. Add mushrooms and stir-fry until browned, about 5 minutes. Stir in shallot and cook until softened, about 1 minute.

4 Stir together broth and cornstarch in cup until smooth, then add to skillet. Cook, stirring constantly, until sauce thickens and boils, about 1 minute. Reduce heat to low; return steak to skillet and stir-fry until heated through, about 1 minute. Stir in sour cream, pepper, and remaining ¼ teaspoon of salt and cook just until heated through (do not boil). Serve with noodles.

9 PointsPlus® value™ Per Serving

PER SERVING (1 ½ cups stroganoff + ¾ cup noodles): *270 grams, 342 Cal, 7 g Total Fat, 2 g Sat Fat, 0 g Trans Fat, 38 mg Chol, 382 mg Sod, 41 g Carb, 4 g Sugar, 6 g Fib, 30 g Prot, 71 mg Calc.*

Thai Beef and Vegetable Curry

SERVES 4

▲ **1 pound boneless sirloin steak, trimmed and thinly sliced**

1 teaspoon canola oil

▲ **¹/₂ pound green beans, trimmed and cut into 1-inch pieces**

▲ **1 red bell pepper, thinly sliced**

▲ **1 onion, thinly sliced**

2 tablespoons water

1 tablespoon plus 1 teaspoon Thai red curry paste

¹/₂ cup light (reduced-fat) coconut milk

▲ **¹/₂ cup reduced-sodium beef broth**

1 tablespoon reduced-sodium Asian fish sauce

1 (8.8-ounce) package cooked brown rice (about 1 ³/₄ cups)

2 tablespoons chopped dry-roasted unsalted peanuts

1 Spray large nonstick skillet with nonstick spray and set over medium-high heat. Add steak and stir-fry until browned, about 3 minutes. Transfer to plate.

2 Heat oil in same skillet over medium-high heat. Add beans, bell pepper, onion, and water; stir-fry until vegetables are crisp-tender, about 3 minutes. Add curry paste and cook, stirring constantly, until fragrant, about 15 seconds. Stir in coconut milk, broth, and fish sauce and bring to boil. Cook, stirring often, until sauce is slightly thickened, about 2 minutes.

3 Meanwhile, heat rice according to package directions for microwave.

4 Return steak to skillet and cook, stirring often, until heated through, about 1 minute. Divide rice evenly among 4 serving plates; top evenly with steak mixture. Sprinkle evenly with peanuts.

PER SERVING (1 ¹/₂ cups curry, scant ¹/₂ cup rice, + ¹/₂ tablespoon peanuts): 350 grams, 413 Cal, 13 g Total Fat, 3 g Sat Fat, 0 g Trans Fat, 66 mg Chol, 626 mg Sod, 33 g Carb, 5 g Sugar, 7 g Fib, 41 g Prot, 77 mg Calc.

▲ *Healthy Extra*

Add 1 zucchini, thinly sliced, when you add the green beans, red bell pepper, and onion. And zip up the flavor by stirring in 3 tablespoons coarsely chopped fresh cilantro, if you like.

Beef and Portobello Burgers

▲ **6 ounces portobello mushroom caps**

▲ **12 ounces ground lean beef (7% fat or less)**

2 tablespoons dried whole wheat bread crumbs

¼ teaspoon salt

¼ teaspoon black pepper

1 teaspoon canola oil

¼ cup low-fat mayonnaise

2 tablespoons finely chopped fresh basil

1 garlic clove, minced

4 whole wheat hamburger buns, split

▲ **4 thick tomato slices**

▲ **4 green leaf lettuce leaves**

1 Place mushrooms in food processor; pulse until minced. Transfer mushrooms to large bowl. Add beef, bread crumbs, salt, and pepper and mix well. With damp hands, shape mixture into 4 (½-inch-thick) patties.

2 Heat oil in large nonstick skillet over medium-high heat. Add patties and cook until instant-read thermometer inserted into side of each burger registers 160°F for medium, 5–6 minutes on each side.

3 Meanwhile, stir together mayonnaise, basil, and garlic in small bowl.

4 Place burgers in buns and top evenly with tomato slices, lettuce leaves, and mayonnaise.

PER SERVING *(1 burger): 243 grams, 323 Cal, 10 g Total Fat, 3 g Sat Fat, 0 g Trans Fat, 51 mg Chol, 658 mg Sod, 34 g Carb, 8 g Sugar, 5 g Fib, 24 g Prot, 97 mg Calc.*

Glazed Pork Chops with Poppy Seed Slaw

SERVES 4

3 tablespoons sugar-free peach preserves

1 tablespoon ketchup

▲ 4 (4-ounce) boneless center-cut loin pork chops, about 1/2 inch thick, trimmed

1 teaspoon chili powder

1/2 teaspoon salt

1/4 cup low-fat buttermilk

1/4 cup low-fat mayonnaise

2 tablespoons apple-cider vinegar

1 teaspoon poppy seeds

1/4 teaspoon black pepper

▲ 1 (14-ounce) bag coleslaw mix

▲ 1 scallion, chopped

1 Spray broiler rack with nonstick spray; preheat broiler.

2 Stir together 1 tablespoon of the preserves and the ketchup in small bowl; set aside. Sprinkle pork chops with chili powder and 1/4 teaspoon of the salt. Place chops on prepared broiler rack and broil 4 inches from heat until instant-read thermometer inserted into side of each chop registers 160°F for medium, 3–4 minutes on each side. Brush tops of chops with preserves mixture. Broil until glazed and bubbling, about 1 minute longer.

3 Meanwhile, to make slaw, whisk together buttermilk, mayonnaise, vinegar, poppy seeds, pepper, and remaining 2 tablespoons preserves and 1/4 teaspoon salt in medium bowl. Add coleslaw mix and scallion and toss to coat. Serve pork chops with slaw.

PER SERVING (1 pork chop + 1 cup slaw): 271 grams, 222 Cal, 9 g Total Fat, 2 g Sat Fat, 0 g Trans Fat, 67 mg Chol, 548 mg Sod, 15 g Carb, 3 g Sugar, 3 g Fib, 23 g Prot, 100 mg Calc.

▲ **Healthy Extra**

Add 1 cup shredded radishes to the slaw mixture for bright color and extra peppery flavor.

Indian-Spiced Pork
with Squash Sauté

Indian-Spiced Pork with Squash Sauté

SERVES 4

▲ 1 ¼ pounds pork tenderloin, trimmed and cut into 8 slices

¾ teaspoon salt

¼ teaspoon black pepper

2 teaspoons canola oil

1 garlic clove, chopped

▲ 2 small zucchini, thinly sliced

▲ 2 small yellow squash, thinly sliced

▲ ½ cup chopped red onion

½ teaspoon curry powder

½ teaspoon ground coriander

½ teaspoon ground cumin

1 Place pork slices in single layer between 2 sheets of plastic wrap. With meat mallet or rolling pin, pound each slice to flatten slightly. Sprinkle pork with ½ teaspoon of the salt and the pepper.

2 Heat 1 teaspoon of the oil in large nonstick skillet over medium heat. Add pork and cook until browned and cooked through, 2–3 minutes on each side. Transfer to platter and keep warm.

3 Add remaining 1 teaspoon oil and the garlic to same skillet and cook over medium heat, stirring constantly, until garlic is fragrant, 30 seconds. Add zucchini, yellow squash, and onion. Cover and cook, stirring occasionally, until vegetables are crisp-tender, about 5 minutes. Stir in curry powder, coriander, cumin, and remaining ¼ teaspoon salt. Serve pork with vegetables.

▲ Healthy Extra

Serve this dish with a refreshing cucumber raita: Mix 1 cucumber, peeled, seeded, and chopped, with ¼ cup plain fat-free yogurt and 1 tablespoon chopped fresh mint.

5 PointsPlus value
Per Serving

PER SERVING (2 slices pork + ¾ cup vegetables): 243 grams, 203 Cal, 6 g Total Fat, 2 g Sat Fat, 0 g Trans Fat, 78 mg Chol, 505 mg Sod, 6 g Carb, 3 g Sugar, 2 g Fib, 30 g Prot, 34 mg Calc.

Chipotle-Honey Pork and Corn Kebabs

SERVES 4

1 teaspoon grated lime zest

2 tablespoons lime juice

1 tablespoon honey

1 chipotle en adobo, minced

▲ 1 (1-pound) pork tenderloin, trimmed and cut into 12 chunks

½ teaspoon salt

¼ teaspoon black pepper

▲ 2 ears corn, shucked and each cut into 4 pieces

▲ 1 red bell pepper, cut into 16 pieces

▲ Healthy Extra

Cut 1 green bell pepper into 16 pieces and thread onto skewers with the other ingredients. Serve each kebab with steamed red quinoa (⅔ cup cooked quinoa per serving will increase the **PointsPlus** value by **3**).

1 Spray broiler rack with nonstick spray; preheat broiler.

2 Stir together lime zest and juice, honey, and chipotle in small bowl; set aside. Sprinkle pork with salt and black pepper. Thread pork, corn, and bell pepper alternately onto 4 (12-inch) metal skewers. Place skewers on prepared broiler rack and broil 5 inches from heat until lightly browned, about 4 minutes on each side.

3 Brush tops of kebabs with half of the honey mixture. Broil until glazed, about 1 minute. Turn kebabs and brush with remaining honey mixture; broil until glazed and pork is no longer pink in center, about 1 minute longer.

PER SERVING (1 kebab): 174 grams, 216 Cal, 4 g Total Fat, 1 g Sat Fat, 0 g Trans Fat, 62 mg Chol, 385 mg Sod, 21 g Carb, 8 g Sugar, 3 g Fib, 25 g Prot, 11 mg Calc.

Moroccan Lamb Chops with Spiced Chickpeas

1 garlic clove, minced

1 teaspoon ground cumin

¾ teaspoon salt

½ teaspoon paprika

Pinch cayenne

▲ 4 (5-ounce) bone-in loin lamb chops, about 1 inch thick, trimmed

2 teaspoons olive oil

▲ 1 onion, chopped

▲ 1 red bell pepper, chopped

▲ 1 (15 ½-ounce) can chickpeas, rinsed and drained

▲ 2 plum tomatoes, chopped

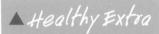

▲ Healthy Extra

Add 1 medium zucchini, diced, with the bell pepper in step 3.

1 Stir together garlic, cumin, salt, paprika, and cayenne in small bowl. Sprinkle lamb with 2 teaspoons of the spice mixture. Reserve remaining spice mixture.

2 Heat 1 teaspoon of the oil in large nonstick skillet over medium-high heat. Add lamb and cook until instant-read thermometer inserted into side of each chop registers 145°F for medium, 4–5 minutes on each side. Transfer to platter and keep warm.

3 Meanwhile, heat remaining 1 teaspoon oil in medium nonstick skillet over medium heat. Add onion, bell pepper, and remaining spice mixture and cook, stirring often, until vegetables are softened, about 3 minutes. Add chickpeas and tomatoes and cook, stirring often, until heated through, about 3 minutes longer. Serve lamb with chickpea mixture.

PER SERVING (1 lamb chop + ¾ cup chickpea mixture): 262 grams, 239 Cal, 8 g Total Fat, 2 g Sat Fat, 0 g Trans Fat, 58 mg Chol, 714 mg Sod, 21 g Carb, 6 g Sugar, 6 g Fib, 20 g Prot, 50 mg Calc.

Lamb Kebabs with Yogurt-Mint Sauce

▲ **1 ½ cups plain fat-free yogurt**

2 tablespoons chopped fresh mint

1 teaspoon ground cumin

1 garlic clove, minced

1 pound boneless leg of lamb, trimmed and cut into 12 chunks

½ teaspoon salt

½ teaspoon black pepper

▲ **2 small zucchini, cut into 8 chunks**

▲ **2 small yellow squash, cut into 8 chunks**

▲ *Healthy Extra*

Make a salad with 2 ripe tomatoes, cut into wedges, ½ of an English (seedless) cucumber, thinly sliced, and ¼ cup of fresh mint leaves sprinkled with 1 tablespoon red-wine vinegar and salt and black pepper to taste.

1 If using wooden skewers, soak 8 (8-inch) wooden skewers in water 15 minutes. Spray broiler rack with nonstick spray; preheat broiler.

2 Stir together yogurt, mint, cumin, and garlic in large bowl. Transfer ¾ cup of the yogurt mixture to small bowl; cover and refrigerate until ready to serve. Sprinkle lamb with salt and pepper. Add lamb to yogurt mixture remaining in large bowl and toss to coat.

3 Thread lamb, zucchini, and yellow squash alternately onto skewers. Discard any yogurt mixture remaining in large bowl. Place skewers on prepared broiler rack and broil 5 inches from heat, turning occasionally, until instant-read thermometer inserted into chunk of lamb registers 145°F for medium, about 10 minutes. Serve kebabs with yogurt sauce.

8 PointsPlus® value ™ Per Serving

PER SERVING *(2 kebabs + 3 tablespoons sauce): 227 grams, 324 Cal, 13 g Total Fat, 5 g Sat Fat, 0 g Trans Fat, 121 mg Chol, 464 mg Sod, 12 g Carb, 9 g Sugar, 2 g Fib, 38 g Prot, 224 mg Calc.*

Lamb Kebabs with Yogurt-Mint Sauce

Dijon-Glazed Chicken and Tomatoes

▲ ½ cup quick-cooking brown rice

▲ 4 (5-ounce) skinless boneless chicken breasts

2 teaspoons olive oil

¾ teaspoon salt

¼ teaspoon plus ⅛ teaspoon black pepper

▲ 4 plum tomatoes, each cut lengthwise in half

1 tablespoon plus 1 teaspoon Dijon mustard

2 ½ teaspoons chopped fresh tarragon

2 tablespoons chopped walnuts

▲ Healthy Extra

Serve the chicken with a microwave-steamed 12-ounce bag of frozen broccoli and cauliflower florets.

1 Spray broiler rack with nonstick spray; preheat broiler.

2 Prepare rice according to package directions, omitting salt if desired.

3 Brush chicken with 1 teaspoon of the oil; sprinkle with ½ teaspoon of the salt and ¼ teaspoon of the pepper. Brush cut sides of tomatoes with remaining 1 teaspoon oil and sprinkle with remaining ¼ teaspoon salt and ⅛ teaspoon pepper. Stir together mustard and 1 ½ teaspoons of the tarragon in small bowl; set aside.

4 Place chicken and tomatoes, cut-sides up, on prepared broiler rack. Broil 4 inches from heat until chicken is lightly browned, about 5 minutes. Turn chicken and brush with mustard mixture. Broil until chicken is cooked through and tomatoes are very tender, 3–4 minutes longer.

5 Stir walnuts into rice. Divide chicken, tomatoes, and rice mixture evenly among 4 serving plates. Sprinkle chicken and tomatoes with remaining 1 teaspoon tarragon.

PER SERVING (1 chicken breast, 2 tomato halves, + ½ cup rice mixture): 290 grams, 304 Cal, 9 g Total Fat, 2 g Sat Fat, 0 g Trans Fat, 78 mg Chol, 628 mg Sod, 23 g Carb, 2 g Sugar, 2 g Fib, 32 g Prot, 35 mg Calc.

Provençal Chicken and Vegetables

SERVES 4

2 teaspoons olive oil

▲ *4 (5-ounce) skinless boneless chicken breasts*

2 teaspoons dried herbes de Provence

3/4 teaspoon salt

1/4 teaspoon plus 1/8 teaspoon red pepper flakes

▲ *2 large zucchini, thinly sliced*

2 garlic cloves, minced

▲ *2 plum tomatoes, chopped*

4 tablespoons grated Parmesan cheese

▲ Healthy Extra

Add a 5-ounce package of baby spinach to the vegetable mixture just before removing from the heat.

1 Heat 1 teaspoon of the oil in large nonstick skillet over medium-high heat. Sprinkle chicken with herbes de Provence, 1/2 teaspoon of the salt, and 1/4 teaspoon of the pepper flakes. Place in skillet and cook, turning occasionally, until cooked through, 8–10 minutes. Transfer chicken to plate and keep warm.

2 Heat remaining 1 teaspoon oil in same skillet over medium-high heat. Add zucchini and cook, covered, stirring occasionally, until crisp-tender, about 4 minutes. Add garlic and cook, stirring constantly, until fragrant, about 30 seconds. Add tomatoes and cook, stirring often, until heated through, about 2 minutes longer. Stir in remaining 1/4 teaspoon salt and 1/8 teaspoon pepper flakes. Divide chicken and vegetables evenly among 4 serving plates; sprinkle evenly with Parmesan.

PER SERVING *(1 chicken breast, 3/4 cup vegetables, + 1 tablespoon cheese): 265 grams, 228 Cal, 7 g Total Fat, 2 g Sat Fat, 0 g Trans Fat, 83 mg Chol, 599 mg Sod, 7 g Carb, 4 g Sugar, 2 g Fib, 33 g Prot, 100 mg Calc.*

Grilled "Béarnaise" Chicken

1 large shallot, minced

1/4 cup chopped fresh tarragon

2 tablespoons red-wine vinegar

2 teaspoons olive oil

1/2 teaspoon salt

1/2 teaspoon coarsely ground black pepper

▲ 4 (5-ounce) skinless boneless chicken breasts

1 Spray grill rack with nonstick spray. Preheat grill to medium-high or prepare medium-high fire.

2 Combine all ingredients except chicken in shallow dish; add chicken and turn to coat.

3 Remove chicken from marinade; discard marinade. Place chicken on grill rack and grill, turning often, until chicken is cooked through, 8–10 minutes.

PER SERVING (1 chicken breast): 132 grams, 184 Cal, 6 g Total Fat, 1 g Sat Fat, 0 g Trans Fat, 78 mg Chol, 361 mg Sod, 2 g Carb, 0 g Sugar, 0 g Fib, 29 g Prot, 29 mg Calc.

▲ **Healthy Extra**

To turn the chicken into a salad, toss mixed greens, tomato wedges, and sliced cucumbers with lemon juice and salt and pepper to taste. Place chicken on top of the salad.

Pesto Chicken and Mushroom Kebabs

SERVES 4

1 cup packed fresh flat-leaf parsley leaves

2 tablespoons grated Parmesan cheese

2 tablespoons sliced almonds

2 teaspoons fresh rosemary

2 teaspoons extra-virgin olive oil

1 garlic clove, chopped

⅛ teaspoon plus ¼ teaspoon salt

⅛ teaspoon plus ¼ teaspoon black pepper

⅓ cup plus 1 tablespoon water

2 tablespoons low-fat mayonnaise

▲ 1 ¼ pounds skinless boneless chicken breasts, cut into 12 chunks

▲ 16 large mushrooms

1 Spray broiler rack with nonstick spray; preheat broiler.

2 To make pesto, place parsley, Parmesan, almonds, rosemary, oil, garlic, ⅛ teaspoon of the salt, and ⅛ teaspoon of the pepper in food processor; pulse to chop. With motor running, gradually pour water through feed tube and process until smooth. Transfer ⅓ cup plus 1 tablespoon of the pesto to small bowl and stir in mayonnaise. Cover and refrigerate until ready to serve.

3 Transfer remaining pesto to large bowl; stir in remaining ¼ teaspoon salt and ¼ teaspoon pepper. Add chicken and mushrooms and toss to coat.

4 Thread chicken and mushrooms alternately onto 4 (12-inch) metal skewers. Discard any pesto remaining in large bowl. Place skewers on prepared broiler rack and broil 5 inches from heat, turning occasionally, until chicken is cooked through, 8–10 minutes. Serve kebabs with pesto mayonnaise.

PER SERVING *(1 kebab + 2 tablespoons sauce): 193 grams, 242 Cal, 9 g Total Fat, 2 g Sat Fat, 0 g Trans Fat, 81 mg Chol, 404 mg Sod, 6 g Carb, 2 g Sugar, 1 g Fib, 33 g Prot, 89 mg Calc.*

▲ Healthy Extra

Serve the kebabs on a bed of quick-cooking barley (⅔ cooked barley per serving will increase the **PointsPlus** value by **3**).

Soba Chicken
Noodle Bowl

Soba Chicken Noodle Bowl

SERVES ~~4~~ 6

▲ **6 ounces thin soba noodles**

▲ **4 cups reduced-sodium chicken broth**

2 cups water

▲ **12 ounces skinless boneless chicken breasts, cut into ¾-inch chunks**

▲ **6 shiitake mushroom caps, sliced**

4 (⅛-inch-thick) slices peeled fresh ginger

3 tablespoons reduced-sodium soy sauce

▲ **½ cup snow peas, cut diagonally into ½-inch-wide strips**

▲ **½ cup thawed frozen baby peas**

▲ **2 cups packed baby spinach**

▲ **1 scallion, minced**

1 Cook noodles according to package directions, omitting salt if desired. Drain and keep warm.

2 Meanwhile, combine broth, water, chicken, mushrooms, ginger, and soy sauce in large saucepan; bring to boil over high heat. Reduce heat and simmer until chicken is almost cooked through, about 6 minutes. Add snow peas, baby peas, and spinach and cook until snow peas are crisp-tender, about 2 minutes. Stir in noodles. Remove and discard ginger. Ladle soup evenly into ~~4~~ 6 serving bowls; sprinkle with scallion.

 PER SERVING (about 2 cups): 435 grams, 214 Cal, 3 g Total Fat, 1 g Sat Fat, 0 g Trans Fat, 31 mg Chol, 594 mg Sod, 30 g Carb, 2 g Sugar, 2 g Fib, 21 g Prot, 39 mg Calc.

▲ Healthy Extra

Toss in a generous handful of fresh bean spouts when adding the noodles to the soup in step 2.

Chicken and Tomatillo Soft Tacos

SERVES 4

1 teaspoon olive oil

▲ *1 pound chicken tenders, each cut crosswise in half*

⅛ teaspoon salt

¼ teaspoon black pepper

▲ *1 (28-ounce) can tomatillos, rinsed and drained*

▲ *1 small onion, chopped*

⅓ cup fresh cilantro leaves

2 garlic cloves, chopped

▲ *1 jalapeño pepper, halved lengthwise and seeded*

8 (7-inch) whole wheat tortillas, warmed

▲ *1 cup shredded romaine lettuce*

▲ *2 tomatoes, chopped*

½ cup crumbled queso fresco cheese

1 Heat oil in large nonstick skillet over medium-high heat. Sprinkle chicken with salt and black pepper. Place in skillet and cook, stirring occasionally, until cooked through, 4–5 minutes. Transfer to plate.

2 Meanwhile, combine tomatillos, onion, cilantro, garlic, and jalapeño in blender; puree until smooth. Add tomatillo mixture to same skillet and bring to boil over high heat. Reduce heat and simmer, stirring occasionally, until slightly thickened, about 3 minutes. Return chicken to skillet and cook until heated through, about 1 minute.

3 Top each tortilla evenly with chicken mixture, lettuce, tomato, and queso fresco. Fold each taco in half and serve at once.

PER SERVING (2 tacos): 320 grams, 406 Cal, 14 g Total Fat, 3 g Sat Fat, 0 g Trans Fat, 73 mg Chol, 744 mg Sod, 45 g Carb, 7 g Sugar, 24 g Fib, 43 g Prot, 117 mg Calc.

▲ **Healthy Extra**

Serve tacos with a Mexican-style salad made with chopped iceberg lettuce, halved cherry tomatoes, chopped red onion, and minced pickled jalapeño, and lime juice to taste.

Buffalo Chicken Burgers with Blue Cheese Dressing

▲ **1 pound ground skinless chicken breast**

▲ **2 tablespoons minced scallions, white parts only**

1 tablespoon dried whole wheat bread crumbs

1/2 teaspoon salt

1/2 teaspoon hot pepper sauce

1 teaspoon canola oil

▲ **1/4 cup plain fat-free yogurt**

1 tablespoon low-fat mayonnaise

▲ **1 small celery stalk with leaves, minced**

2 tablespoons reduced-fat blue cheese crumbles

4 whole wheat hamburger buns, split and warmed

▲ **4 lettuce leaves**

1 Combine chicken, scallions, bread crumbs, salt, and pepper sauce in large bowl and mix well. With damp hands, shape mixture into 4 (1/2-inch-thick) patties.

2 Heat oil in large nonstick skillet over medium-high heat. Add patties and reduce heat to medium. Partially cover and cook until instant-read thermometer inserted into side of each burger registers 165°F, 10–12 minutes.

3 Meanwhile, to make dressing, stir together yogurt, mayonnaise, celery, and blue cheese in small bowl.

4 Place burgers in buns and top evenly with dressing and lettuce leaves.

 PER SERVING *(1 burger): 239 grams, 314 Cal, 8 g Total Fat, 2 g Sat Fat, 0 g Trans Fat, 65 mg Chol, 764 mg Sod, 30 g Carb, 7 g Sugar, 4 g Fib, 30 g Prot, 146 mg Calc.*

▲ *Healthy Extra*

Add a thick tomato slice to each burger and serve with crunchy carrot sticks.

Turkey Cutlets with Marsala Mushroom Sauce

SERVES 4

2 teaspoons olive oil

▲ 4 (¼-pound) turkey breast cutlets

¾ teaspoon salt

½ teaspoon black pepper

▲ 1 (10-ounce) package sliced cremini mushrooms

2 tablespoons minced shallots

1 teaspoon all-purpose flour

▲ ⅔ cup reduced-sodium chicken broth

⅓ cup dry Marsala wine

▲ *Healthy Extra*

Serve with steamed green beans and brown rice (⅔ cup cooked brown rice for each serving will increase the **PointsPlus** value by 3).

1 Heat 1 teaspoon of the oil in large nonstick skillet over medium heat. Sprinkle turkey with ½ teaspoon of the salt and ¼ teaspoon of the pepper. Place in skillet and cook, turning once, until lightly browned, 4–6 minutes. Transfer to plate.

2 Heat remaining 1 teaspoon oil in same skillet over medium-high heat. Add mushrooms and cook, stirring occasionally, until beginning to brown, 4–5 minutes. Add shallots and cook, stirring often, until shallots are softened, about 1 minute. Stir in flour and remaining ¼ teaspoon salt and ¼ teaspoon pepper.

3 Stir in broth and Marsala; bring to boil. Return turkey and any accumulated juices to skillet. Reduce heat and simmer, turning turkey occasionally, until turkey is cooked through and sauce is slightly thickened, 2–3 minutes longer.

5 PointsPlus value
Per Serving

PER SERVING (1 turkey cutlet + ⅓ cup mushroom sauce): 175 grams, 207 Cal, 3 g Total Fat, 0 g Sat Fat, 0 g Trans Fat, 45 mg Chol, 636 mg Sod, 9 g Carb, 3 g Sugar, 0 g Fib, 31 g Prot, 24 mg Calc.

Moussaka-Style Turkey with Eggplant

▲ **1 large eggplant (1 ¹/₂ pounds), cut crosswise into 12 (¹/₂-inch-thick) rounds**

1 teaspoon olive oil

▲ **1 small onion, finely chopped**

1 garlic clove, minced

▲ **12 ounces ground skinless turkey breast**

¹/₂ teaspoon salt

¹/₄ teaspoon black pepper

▲ **1 (8-ounce) can tomato sauce**

¹/₂ teaspoon dried oregano

¹/₄ teaspoon ground cinnamon

4 tablespoons crumbled reduced-fat feta cheese

1 Spray broiler rack with olive oil nonstick spray; preheat broiler.

2 Place eggplant slices on prepared broiler rack; lightly spray with olive oil nonstick spray. Broil 5 inches from heat until lightly browned, 5–6 minutes. Remove pan from broiler; turn eggplant over and lightly spray with olive oil nonstick spray. Return to broiler and broil until eggplant is lightly browned and tender, 5–6 minutes longer.

3 Meanwhile, heat oil in large nonstick skillet over medium heat. Add onion and garlic and cook, covered, stirring occasionally, until onion is softened, about 3 minutes. Add turkey, salt, and pepper and cook, breaking turkey apart with wooden spoon, until turkey is no longer pink, about 6 minutes. Stir in tomato sauce, oregano, and cinnamon and bring to boil. Reduce heat and simmer until slightly thickened, about 3 minutes.

4 Divide eggplant slices evenly among 4 serving plates; top evenly with turkey mixture and sprinkle with feta.

PER SERVING (1 plate): 329 grams, 175 Cal, 4 g Total Fat, 1 g Sat Fat, 0 g Trans Fat, 36 mg Chol, 758 mg Sod, 13 g Carb, 6 g Sugar, 6 g Fib, 25 g Prot, 55 mg Calc.

Turkey Sausage, Tomato, and Basil Pizza

1 (2 ½-ounce) link Italian turkey sausage, casing removed

1 (10-ounce) prebaked whole wheat thin pizza crust

¾ cup shredded part-skim mozzarella cheese

▲ *1 cup cherry tomatoes, halved*

2 tablespoons chopped fresh basil

1 Preheat oven to 450°F. Spray baking sheet with nonstick spray.

2 Cook sausage in medium nonstick skillet over medium-high heat, breaking sausage apart with wooden spoon, until sausage is no longer pink, about 6 minutes.

3 Place crust on prepared baking sheet. Top crust evenly with mozzarella, sausage, and tomatoes. Bake until cheese is melted and bubbly, about 8 minutes. Sprinkle with basil and cut into 4 wedges.

PER SERVING *(1 wedge): 155 grams, 264 Cal, 8 g Total Fat, 3 g Sat Fat, 0 g Trans Fat, 22 mg Chol, 526 mg Sod, 32 g Carb, 1 g Sugar, 4 g Fib, 14 g Prot, 186 mg Calc.*

▲ *Healthy Extra*

Add 1 cup lightly packed baby arugula to pizza before topping with mozzarella, sausage, and tomatoes.

The List Goes High Tech

If you prefer going old school, using pen and paper to make up your weekly list—no worries. But if time is an issue and you're comfortable with a desktop, laptop, or smart phone, consider going high tech.

■ **Make a Master List.** Create a standard shopping list and save it on your computer or smart phone. Print as needed, highlighting the items you need to pick up at the store. If using a smart phone, there's no need to print, simply highlight the items you need. Reap even greater efficiency by organizing your list to coincide with the layout of your market.

■ **There's an App for That.** Try using a grocery list app—many are available as inexpensive or free downloads. These range from standard list-making tools to versions that let you create custom lists for several stores and some will even calculate the cost of everything on your list. If you're tech savvy, an app can make grocery shopping more efficient and fun.

■ **Be Supermarket Savvy.** Check your grocery store's website for interactive shopping help. Some sites let you create lists based on the store layout or create a shopping list from downloaded recipes. You can sign up to receive coupons and special offers by email, too.

■ **Think the New "Clip."** If you're a fan of coupons, you can go online and find a coupon for almost anything. You're no longer limited to offerings from circulars or the Sunday papers. There are sites that let you download and print coupons directly and others that mail paper coupons to you. Also check the websites of brands you buy often. Sometimes they have downloadable coupons or you can sign up to receive coupons by email.

■ **Shop from Home.** In some parts of the country, supermarkets offer online shopping and delivery for a small fee. These sites let you create a shopping list or use one of your previous orders as a list to shop from.

Peppered Tuna with Lemongrass Vinaigrette

SERVES 4

¼ *cup finely chopped fresh cilantro*

2 tablespoons lime juice

2 tablespoons seasoned rice vinegar

1 tablespoon minced lemongrass

2 teaspoons reduced-sodium soy sauce

2 teaspoons olive oil

1 garlic clove, minced

▲ *4 (5-ounce) tuna steaks*

2 teaspoons coarsely ground black pepper

½ *teaspoon salt*

▲ *4 cups mixed baby greens*

1 Hass avocado, pitted, peeled, and cut into ½-*inch chunks*

1 To make vinaigrette, stir together cilantro, lime juice, vinegar, lemongrass, soy sauce, oil, and garlic in small bowl.

2 Spray large nonstick skillet with nonstick spray and set over medium-high heat. Sprinkle tuna with pepper and salt. Place in skillet and cook 2–3 minutes on each side for medium-rare.

3 Transfer tuna to cutting board and let stand 5 minutes. Slice tuna into ¼-inch-thick slices. Divide baby greens and avocado evenly among 4 serving plates; top evenly with tuna and drizzle with vinaigrette.

PER SERVING *(1 plate): 280 grams, 243 Cal, 11 g Total Fat, 2 g Sat Fat, 0 g Trans Fat, 51 mg Chol, 459 mg Sod, 9 g Carb, 2 g Sugar, 5 g Fib, 29 g Prot, 33 mg Calc.*

▲ **Healthy Extra**

Quinoa makes a quick and easy side to serve with these flavorful tuna steaks. (⅔ cup cooked quinoa per serving will increase the **PointsPlus** value by **3**).

Peppered Tuna with Lemongrass Vinaigrette

Tilapia with Prosciutto and Artichokes

SERVES 4

▲ **4 (5-ounce) tilapia fillets**

4 thin slices prosciutto (about 2 ounces)

8 fresh sage leaves

½ teaspoon black pepper

2 teaspoons olive oil

▲ **¾ cup reduced-sodium chicken broth**

2 teaspoons cornstarch

▲ **2 (14-ounce) cans quartered artichokes, rinsed and drained**

1 teaspoon butter

1 tablespoon chopped fresh parsley

1 Cut each tilapia fillet lengthwise in half to make 8 pieces total. Cut each prosciutto slice lengthwise in half. Wrap prosciutto slice crosswise around each piece of fish. Tuck 2 sage leaves underneath each prosciutto slice. Sprinkle fillets with pepper.

2 Heat oil in large nonstick skillet over medium-high heat. Add fillets and cook, in batches, if necessary, turning once, until prosciutto is browned and fish is just opaque, 2–3 minutes on each side. Transfer to platter and keep warm.

3 Whisk together broth and cornstarch in small bowl until blended. Add broth mixture and artichokes to skillet; bring to boil. Cook, stirring occasionally, until mixture simmers and thickens, 2–3 minutes. Remove from heat. Stir in butter and parsley. Spoon artichoke mixture over fish.

PER SERVING (2 pieces tilapia + ½ cup artichoke mixture): 240 grams, 302 Cal, 10 g Total Fat, 3 g Sat Fat, 0 g Trans Fat, 74 mg Chol, 586 mg Sod, 19 g Carb, 0 g Sugar, 12 g Fib, 38 g Prot, 114 mg Calc.

Crumb-Crusted Scallops with Parmesan Tomatoes

SERVES 4

▲ **2 large tomatoes, each cut into 4 (¹/₂-inch-thick) slices**

2 ¹/₂ tablespoons grated Parmesan cheese

¹/₄ cup dried whole wheat bread crumbs

1 tablespoon chopped fresh parsley

2 teaspoons olive oil

Grated zest of 1 lemon

▲ **1 ¹/₄ pounds sea scallops (about 16)**

¹/₄ teaspoon black pepper

1 Spray broiler rack with nonstick spray; preheat broiler.

2 Place tomato slices on prepared broiler rack; top each with about 1 teaspoon Parmesan. Broil 4 inches from heat until tomatoes are tender and cheese is bubbly, 2–3 minutes. Transfer tomatoes to plate and keep warm.

3 Meanwhile, combine bread crumbs, parsley, oil, and lemon zest in large bowl. Add scallops; toss to coat. Place scallops on broiler rack; lightly spray with nonstick spray. Broil 4 inches from heat until lightly browned and opaque in center, 2–3 minutes (do not turn). Serve scallops with tomato slices.

PER SERVING *(about 4 scallops + 2 tomato slices): 290 grams, 316 Cal, 6 g Total Fat, 1 g Sat Fat, 0 g Trans Fat, 112 mg Chol, 655 mg Sod, 17 g Carb, 3 g Sugar, 2 g Fib, 49 g Prot, 135 mg Calc..*

Masala Shrimp Kebabs with Yogurt Sauce

Masala Shrimp Kebabs with Yogurt Sauce

SERVES 4

1 ½ teaspoons chili powder

1 teaspoon garam masala

1 teaspoon canola oil

1 garlic clove, minced

½ teaspoon salt

▲ 1 pound peeled and deveined large shrimp

▲ 1 cup plain fat-free Greek yogurt

2 tablespoons chopped fresh mint

▲ 2 tablespoons minced scallions

Grated zest of 1 lemon

2 (9 x 10-inch) pieces whole wheat lavash-style flatbread

1 Spray broiler rack with nonstick spray; preheat broiler.

2 Stir together chili powder, garam masala, oil, garlic, and ¼ teaspoon of the salt in large bowl; add shrimp and toss to coat. Thread shrimp onto 8 (6-inch) metal skewers. Place skewers on prepared broiler rack and broil 5 inches from heat, turning once, until just opaque throughout, about 5 minutes.

3 Meanwhile, to make sauce, stir together yogurt, mint, scallions, lemon zest, and remaining ¼ teaspoon salt in small bowl. Cut each flatbread in half. Serve shrimp with sauce and flatbread.

PER SERVING *(2 kebabs, ¼ cup sauce, + ½ piece flatbread): 228 grams, 254 Cal, 3 g Total Fat, 0 g Sat Fat, 0 g Trans Fat, 168 mg Chol, 676 mg Sod, 26 g Carb, 3 g Sugar, 3 g Fib, 27 g Prot, 104 mg Calc.*

▲ Healthy Extra

Broil 4 nectarines, each cut in half, pitted, and sprayed with olive oil nonstick spray, alongside shrimp on broiler rack.

Mussels in Carrot-Ginger Broth

SERVES 4

2 teaspoons canola oil

▲ 1 small onion, thinly sliced

▲ 2 medium tomatoes, chopped

1 tablespoon minced peeled fresh ginger

1 garlic clove, minced

¹/₂ teaspoon salt

¹/₄ teaspoon red pepper flakes

2 cups carrot juice

▲ 1 cup reduced-sodium chicken broth

▲ 2 pounds mussels (about 6 dozen), scrubbed and debearded

2 tablespoons chopped fresh tarragon

2 teaspoons lemon juice

1 Heat oil in large deep nonstick skillet over medium heat. Add onion and cook, stirring often, until softened, about 3 minutes. Add tomatoes, ginger, garlic, salt, and pepper flakes; cook, stirring constantly, until tomatoes are softened, about 3 minutes. Add carrot juice and broth; bring to boil. Reduce heat and simmer, covered, 5 minutes.

2 Increase heat to medium-high; add mussels. Cook, covered, until mussels open, about 4 minutes. Discard any mussels that do not open. With slotted spoon, divide mussels evenly among 4 serving bowls. Stir tarragon and lemon juice into broth in skillet. Ladle broth evenly over mussels.

PER SERVING *(about 18 mussels + ²/₃ cup broth): 475 grams, 131 Cal, 4 g Total Fat, 1 g Sat Fat, 0 g Trans Fat, 14 mg Chol, 530 mg Sod, 15 g Carb, 3 g Sugar, 1 g Fib, 9 g Prot, 53 mg Calc.*

▲ Healthy Extra

Serve this bistro dish with a salad of 4 cups chopped curly endive and 1 chopped pear, sprinkled with a little lemon juice.

Mussels in Carrot-Ginger Broth

Salmon and Bok Choy in Thai Curry Broth

SERVES 4

2 teaspoons canola oil

▲ 3 scallions, thinly sliced

2 garlic cloves, minced

1 tablespoon grated peeled fresh ginger

1 teaspoon Thai green curry paste

1/2 teaspoon ground cumin

1/2 teaspoon ground coriander

▲ 3 cups reduced-sodium chicken broth

▲ 3 baby bok choy, quartered lengthwise

▲ 1 pound skinless salmon fillets, cut into 1-inch chunks

1/2 teaspoon salt

Grated zest and juice of 1 lime

2 tablespoons chopped fresh mint

1 Heat oil in large nonstick skillet over medium-high heat. Add scallions, garlic, ginger, curry paste, cumin, and coriander; cook, stirring constantly, until fragrant, 1 minute. Add broth and bok choy; bring to boil. Reduce heat and simmer, stirring often, until bok choy just begins to wilt, 2–3 minutes.

2 Sprinkle salmon with salt. Add salmon and lime zest and juice to broth. Simmer, uncovered, until salmon is just opaque, 2–3 minutes. Remove from heat; stir in mint.

PER SERVING (1 1/2 cups): 370 grams, 256 Cal, 12 g Total Fat, 2 g Sat Fat, 0 g Trans Fat, 72 mg Chol, 481 mg Sod, 7 g Carb, 2 g Sugar, 2 g Fib, 31 g Prot, 41 mg Calc.

▲ Healthy Extra

You can add 1 cup of baby spinach and 1 cup of cooked whole wheat fusilli to the broth along with the salmon in step 2. This will increase the per-serving **PointsPlus** value by **1**.

Bowties with Broccoli Pesto

SERVES 4

- ▲ **8 ounces whole wheat farfalle**
- ▲ **2 cups broccoli florets**
- **3 tablespoons water**
- **1 cup packed fresh basil leaves**
- **2 tablespoons grated Parmesan cheese**
- **2 tablespoons pine nuts**
- **2 garlic cloves, halved**
- **1/2 teaspoon salt**
- **1/4 teaspoon red pepper flakes**
- ▲ **1/4 cup reduced-sodium vegetable broth**
- **2 teaspoons olive oil**
- **Grated zest of 1 lemon**
- ▲ **6 dry-packed sun-dried tomatoes, thinly sliced**

1 Cook farfalle according to package directions, omitting salt if desired; drain and keep warm.

2 Meanwhile, place broccoli and water in medium microwavable dish. Cover and microwave on High until tender, 2–3 minutes; drain. Rinse under cold running water; drain again.

3 To make pesto, place broccoli, basil, Parmesan, 1 tablespoon of the pine nuts, the garlic, salt, and pepper flakes in food processor; pulse until coarsely chopped. Add broth and oil; process until smooth.

4 Combine pasta, pesto, and lemon zest in large serving bowl; toss to coat. Sprinkle with sun-dried tomatoes and remaining 1 tablespoon pine nuts.

PER SERVING (1 1/4 cups): 150 grams, 297 Cal, 8 g Total Fat, 1 g Sat Fat, 0 g Trans Fat, 2 mg Chol, 422 mg Sod, 48 g Carb, 4 g Sugar, 7 g Fib, 11 g Prot, 96 mg Calc.

▲ Healthy Extra

Add 1 cup frozen peas to the pasta during the last 3 minutes of cooking (the per-serving **PointsPlus** value will increase by **1**).

*Caramelized Onion Risotto
with Chickpeas*

Caramelized Onion Risotto with Chickpeas

SERVES 4

2 teaspoons olive oil

▲ 1 sweet onion, halved and thinly sliced

¼ cup water

▲ 1 ½ cups reduced-sodium vegetable broth

2 teaspoons cornstarch

▲ 1 (15 ½-ounce) can chickpeas, rinsed and drained

▲ 1 (9-ounce) package baby spinach

▲ 1 (8.8-ounce) package cooked brown rice (about 1 ¾ cups)

Grated zest and juice of 1 lemon

2 tablespoons chopped fresh dill

¼ cup crumbled reduced-fat feta cheese

1 Heat oil in large nonstick saucepan over medium heat. Add onion and water and cook, stirring often, until onion is deep golden and water evaporates, about 10 minutes.

2 Meanwhile, whisk together broth and cornstarch in small bowl until smooth.

3 Add chickpeas, spinach, and rice to saucepan. Whisk cornstarch mixture and add to chickpea mixture; bring to boil. Cook, stirring often, until spinach wilts and mixture is slightly thickened, about 3 minutes. Stir in lemon zest and juice and dill. Remove from heat; sprinkle with feta.

PER SERVING (1 ¼ cups): 350 grams, 288 Cal, 6 g Total Fat, 1 g Sat Fat, 0 g Trans Fat, 3 mg Chol, 524 mg Sod, 52 g Carb, 7 g Sugar, 10 g Fib, 10 g Prot, 126 mg Calc.

F.Y.I.

When sautéing vegetables in small amounts of oil, adding water or broth, 2 tablespoons at a time, as needed, allows them to cook more quickly and keeps them from sticking to the pan.

Roasted Eggplant and Hummus Tartines

SERVES 4

▲ *1 medium eggplant, cut crosswise into 12 (¹/4-inch-thick) rounds*

▲ *6 ounces portobello mushroom caps*

▲ *2 medium tomatoes, chopped*

▲ *¹/2 small cucumber, diced*

6 Kalamata olives, pitted and chopped

2 tablespoons chopped fresh mint

1 tablespoon apple-cider vinegar

2 teaspoons olive oil

¹/4 teaspoon salt

¹/4 cup prepared hummus

4 (¹/2-inch) slices whole grain country-style bread, toasted (2 ounces each)

▲ *1 cup baby arugula*

1 Spray broiler rack with nonstick spray; preheat broiler. Arrange eggplant and mushrooms in single layer on rack. Lightly spray with olive oil nonstick spray. Broil 5 inches from heat, turning occasionally, until lightly browned and tender, 6–8 minutes. Cut mushrooms into thin slices.

2 Meanwhile, to make salsa, stir together tomatoes, cucumber, olives, mint, vinegar, oil, and salt in large bowl.

3 Spread hummus evenly on toast; top with arugula, eggplant, and mushrooms. Spoon salsa evenly over sandwiches.

PER SERVING *(1 open-face sandwich): 235 grams, 268 Cal, 8 g Total Fat, 1 g Sat Fat, 0 g Trans Fat, 0 mg Chol, 542 mg Sod, 40 g Carb, 9 g Sugar, 11 g Fib, 12 g Prot, 99 mg Calc.*

Tofu, Broccolini, and Cashew Stir-Fry

SERVES 4

▲ **2 (8-ounce) bunches broccolini**

▲ **²⁄₃ cup reduced-sodium vegetable broth**

3 tablespoons reduced-sodium soy sauce

2 tablespoons mirin

1 tablespoon minced peeled fresh ginger

2 teaspoons cornstarch

¹⁄₂ teaspoon Asian (dark) sesame oil

¹⁄₄ teaspoon red pepper flakes

1 garlic clove, chopped

2 teaspoons canola oil

▲ **3 scallions, cut into 3-inch pieces**

▲ **1 (14-ounce) container extra-firm tofu, drained and cut into 1-inch chunks**

2 tablespoons chopped roasted unsalted cashews

1 Bring large saucepan of water to boil. Add broccolini and cook until just crisp-tender, 3 minutes; drain.

2 Meanwhile, whisk together broth, soy sauce, mirin, ginger, cornstarch, sesame oil, pepper flakes, and garlic in small bowl.

3 Heat canola oil in large nonstick skillet over medium-high heat. Add broccolini and scallions and cook, stirring often, until scallions are tender, about 2 minutes. Stir in tofu. Add broth mixture; bring to boil. Cook, stirring often, until sauce is slightly thickened, about 3 minutes. Sprinkle with cashews.

PER SERVING (1 ¹⁄₂ cups): 315 grams, 222 Cal, 10 g Total Fat, 1 g Sat Fat, 0 g Trans Fat, 0 mg Chol, 460 mg Sod, 18 g Carb, 6 g Sugar, 3 g Fib, 14 g Prot, 286 mg Calc.

F.Y.I.

To save on prep time, you can use jarred minced ginger and garlic.

*Zucchini Fritters with
Yogurt-Apricot Sauce*

Zucchini Fritters with Yogurt-Apricot Sauce

▲ ¾ *cup plain fat-free Greek yogurt*

1 tablespoon apricot fruit spread

1 teaspoon curry powder

▲ *2 medium zucchini*

▲ *3 scallions, finely chopped*

▲ *1 large egg*

▲ *1 large egg white*

⅓ cup whole wheat flour

1 teaspoon baking powder

½ teaspoon salt

3 teaspoons canola oil

▲ Healthy Extra

Stir ½ cup shredded carrot into the batter.

1 Stir together yogurt, fruit spread, and curry in small bowl; cover and refrigerate until ready to serve.

2 Shred zucchini on large holes of box grater into large bowl. Spread zucchini on clean kitchen towel. Roll up and squeeze to remove excess liquid. Return zucchini to bowl. Add scallions, egg, egg white, flour, baking powder, and salt; stir to combine.

3 Heat 1 ½ teaspoons of the oil in large nonstick skillet over medium-high heat. Drop batter by heaping tablespoons into skillet to make 6 fritters and cook until browned, 2–3 minutes on each side. Repeat with remaining oil and batter to make total of 12 fritters, removing skillet from heat and spraying with nonstick spray between batches, if needed. Serve fritters with yogurt sauce.

PER SERVING (*3 fritters + 3 tablespoons sauce*): *165 grams, 142 Cal, 5 g Total Fat, 1 g Sat Fat, 0 g Trans Fat, 54 mg Chol, 486 mg Sod, 17 g Carb, 6 g Sugar, 3 g Fib, 9 g Prot, 87 mg Calc.*

4 PointsPlus® value ™ Per Serving

15 MIN

fastest

*Not much time?
These 15-minute
miracles prove
you can make a
healthful, hearty
main dish in a flash.
Simple, delicious,
and easy on the
cook—these recipes
are sure to become
family favorites
you'll make again
and again.*

*Korean-Style Steak
and Kimchi Wraps*

Korean-Style Steak and Kimchi Wraps

- ▲ **1 (1-pound) flank steak, trimmed**

  4 teaspoons reduced-sodium soy sauce

  1 teaspoon Asian (dark) sesame oil

  ¼ teaspoon black pepper

- ▲ **1 (8.8-ounce) package cooked brown rice (about 1 ¾ cups)**

  ¼ cup prepared kimchi

- ▲ **8 leaves Bibb lettuce**

F.Y.I.

Kimchi is a spicy fermented vegetable mixture used as a condiment in Korean dishes. Look for it in the refrigerated section of many supermarkets and Asian markets.

1 Spray broiler rack with nonstick spray; preheat broiler.

2 Brush steak with soy sauce and oil; sprinkle with pepper. Place on prepared broiler rack and broil 4 inches from heat until instant-read thermometer inserted into side of steak registers 145°F for medium, 3–4 minutes on each side. Transfer steak to cutting board and loosely cover with foil; let stand 2–3 minutes. Cut across grain into 16 slices.

3 Meanwhile, heat rice according to package directions for microwave.

4 Divide steak, rice, and kimchi evenly among lettuce leaves. Roll up and serve at once.

PER SERVING (2 wraps): 210 grams, 283 Cal, 8 g Total Fat, 3 g Sat Fat, 0 g Trans Fat, 42 mg Chol, 478 mg Sod, 23 g Carb, 1 g Sugar, 3 g Fib, 27 g Prot, 36 mg Calc.

7 PointsPlus© value™ Per Serving

Steak and Beet Salad with Horseradish Dressing

SERVES 4

▲ **1 (1-pound) sirloin steak, trimmed**

¾ teaspoon salt

½ teaspoon black pepper

▲ **¼ cup fat-free sour cream**

1 tablespoon prepared horseradish

1 teaspoon water

▲ **2 cups radicchio, torn into bite-size pieces**

▲ **2 cups baby arugula**

▲ **2 precooked medium beets, cut into thin strips**

1 Spray large nonstick skillet with nonstick spray and set over medium-high heat. Sprinkle steak with ½ teaspoon of the salt and ¼ teaspoon of the pepper. Place in skillet and cook until instant-read thermometer inserted into center of steak registers 145°F for medium, 3–4 minutes on each side. Transfer steak to cutting board and loosely cover with foil; let stand 2–3 minutes. Cut across grain into 16 slices.

2 Meanwhile, to make dressing, stir together sour cream, horseradish, and water in small bowl.

3 Toss together radicchio, arugula, beets, and remaining ¼ teaspoon salt and ¼ teaspoon pepper in large bowl.

4 Divide salad evenly among 4 serving plates, top with steak, and drizzle with dressing.

PER SERVING (4 slices steak, 1 ½ cups salad, + 1 tablespoon dressing): 190 grams, 191 Cal, 5 g Total Fat, 2 g Sat Fat, 0 g Trans Fat, 51 mg Chol, 568 mg Sod, 7 g Carb, 3 g Sugar, 1 g Fib, 28 g Prot, 68 mg Calc.

F.Y.I.

Look for precooked beets in vacuum-sealed packages in many large supermarkets. If you can't find them, you can use canned beets in this recipe instead.

Steak Pizzaiola with Polenta

SERVES 4

- ▲ **1 (16-ounce) tube refrigerated fat-free plain polenta, cut into 8 rounds**
- ▲ **1 (1-pound) sirloin steak, trimmed**
  ¹/₂ teaspoon salt
  ¹/₂ teaspoon black pepper
- ▲ **1 (8-ounce) package sliced cremini mushrooms**
  2 tablespoons sweet vermouth
- ▲ **1 (8-ounce) can no-salt-added tomato sauce**
  Chopped fresh basil (optional)

Healthy Extra

Cook 1 cup diced red bell pepper along with the mushrooms.

1 Preheat broiler. Spray large baking sheet with nonstick spray. Arrange polenta in single layer on baking sheet. Broil polenta 4 inches from heat until lightly browned and heated through, 6–8 minutes.

2 Meanwhile, spray large ridged grill pan with nonstick spray and set over medium-high heat. Sprinkle steak with ¹/₄ teaspoon of the salt and ¹/₄ teaspoon of the pepper. Place in grill pan and cook until instant-read thermometer inserted into center of steak registers 145°F for medium, 3–4 minutes on each side. Transfer steak to cutting board and loosely cover with foil; let stand 2–3 minutes. Cut across grain into 16 slices.

3 At same time, spray medium nonstick skillet with nonstick spray and set over medium-high heat. Add mushrooms and cook, stirring often, until tender, about 5 minutes. Add vermouth and cook 1 minute. Stir in tomato sauce and remaining ¹/₄ teaspoon salt and ¹/₄ teaspoon pepper. Bring to boil, reduce heat, and simmer 3 minutes.

4 Divide polenta evenly among 4 serving plates, top evenly with steak, and spoon sauce over steak. Sprinkle with basil, if using.

PER SERVING (4 slices steak, 2 slices polenta, + ¹/₃ cup sauce): 270 grams, 287 Cal, 6 g Total Fat, 2 g Sat Fat, 0 g Trans Fat, 49 mg Chol, 707 mg Sod, 24 g Carb, 5 g Sugar, 2 g Fib, 30 g Prot, 36 mg Calc.

Steak Salad with Spinach and Oranges

▲ **1 (1-pound) sirloin steak, trimmed**

1 teaspoon ground cumin

3/4 teaspoon salt

1/2 teaspoon black pepper

▲ **2 navel oranges**

▲ **1 (6-ounce) package baby spinach**

▲ **1 cup cherry tomatoes, halved**

3 tablespoons lemon juice

1 teaspoon extra-virgin olive oil

2 tablespoons chopped dry-roasted salted almonds

> ## F.Y.I.
>
> **Instead of navel oranges,** you can make this salad with 2 clementines, peeled and separated into segments.

1 Spray large ridged grill pan with nonstick spray and set over medium-high heat. Sprinkle steak with cumin, 1/2 teaspoon of the salt, and 1/4 teaspoon of the pepper. Place in grill pan and cook until instant-read thermometer inserted into center of steak registers 145°F for medium, 3–4 minutes on each side. Transfer steak to cutting board and loosely cover with foil; let stand 2–3 minutes. Cut across grain into 16 slices.

2 Meanwhile, to make salad, with sharp knife, peel oranges, removing all white pith. Cut oranges into rounds; cut rounds into quarters. Place oranges in large bowl. Add spinach, tomatoes, lemon juice, oil, and remaining 1/4 teaspoon salt and 1/4 teaspoon pepper; toss to coat.

3 Divide salad evenly among 4 serving plates and top evenly with steak. Sprinkle evenly with almonds and serve at once.

PER SERVING (4 slices steak, 2 cups salad + 1/2 tablespoon almonds): 265 grams, 257 Cal, 9 g Total Fat, 2 g Sat Fat, 0 g Trans Fat, 49 mg Chol, 576 mg Sod, 5 g Carb, 7 g Sugar, 5 g Fib, 29 g Prot, 99 mg Calc.

Delegate the Small Stuff

The fastest way to get anything done is to enlist help. Use these tricks to put everyone in the family—your kids and spouse—to pitch in so dinner together will be a pleasure for everyone.

■ **Teach Them Young.** Even young children can help get dinner on the table, saving you time and making them feel like they are contributing to the family. Enlist small ones to put bread and napkins on the table. Have them do tasks that don't require using sharp tools. They can dry greens in a salad spinner, measure ingredients for a salad dressing, or tear off the leaves of fresh herbs.

■ **Involve Everyone.** Recruit older children to set the table, peel and chop vegetables, wash salad greens, or grate cheese. Let them know how much you value their assistance and you'll have a team of helpers every night.

■ **There's No Time Like the Present.** Either right after dinner or some time before bed, ask for help to get ready for tomorrow's breakfast and lunch. Have kids set out bowls or plates and silverware, set out cereal or the pan needed to cook the oatmeal or make the eggs. If there are lunches to be packed, doing as much prep the night before will ensure a less stressed morning. Assemble sandwiches and transfer soups or salads into individual containers so they're ready to drop into the lunch box the next day. Every second saved counts in the morning rush.

■ **Set Up the Rules.** Make it a house rule that if you use the last of anything, you have to add it to the master grocery shopping list. Once you forget to buy someone's favorite brand of breakfast cereal, the incentive to write it down will be reinforced.

■ **Encourage a Team Mentality.** When everyone is through eating, have each family member bring their dishes to the kitchen and help get any serving bowls and utensils into the kitchen for clean up.

Fig-Glazed Pork Chops with Green Beans

▲ **4 (4-ounce) boneless center-cut loin pork chops, trimmed**

¾ teaspoon salt

½ teaspoon black pepper

2 tablespoons fig jam

½ cup water

▲ **1 pound pre-trimmed fresh green beans**

2 tablespoons grated Parmesan cheese

1 Spray broiler rack with nonstick spray; preheat broiler.

2 Sprinkle pork with ½ teaspoon of the salt and ¼ teaspoon of the pepper. Place on prepared broiler rack and broil 4 inches from heat until instant-read thermometer inserted into center of each chop registers 160°F for medium, 3–4 minutes on each side. Top chops evenly with jam; broil until jam is bubbling, about 1 minute.

3 Meanwhile, bring water to boil in large skillet. Add beans, cover, and cook until beans are just crisp-tender, about 5 minutes. Drain and toss with Parmesan and remaining ¼ teaspoon salt and ¼ teaspoon pepper. Serve pork chops with beans.

▲ Healthy Extra

Serve the pork chops and green beans with a side of whole wheat linguine. A ½-cup serving of cooked whole wheat linguine will increase the **PointsPlus** value by **2**.

PER SERVING (1 pork chop + 1 cup green beans): 195 grams, 204 Cal, 7 g Total Fat, 2 g Sat Fat, 0 g Trans Fat, 68 mg Chol, 527 mg Sod, 12 g Carb, 4 g Sugar, 4 g Fib, 24 g Prot, 90 mg Calc.

*Fig-Glazed Pork Chops
with Green Beans*

Pork Chops with Asian Pineapple Salsa

SERVES 4

 4 (4-ounce) boneless center-cut loin pork chops, trimmed

¹/₂ teaspoon salt

¹/₄ teaspoon black pepper

 1 cup pre-cut fresh pineapple chunks or canned unsweetened pineapple chunks, drained

1 shallot, minced

1 tablespoon Asian fish sauce

1 teaspoon brown sugar

¹/₄ cup packed fresh cilantro leaves

Pinch red pepper flakes

 1 (8.8-ounce) package cooked brown rice (about 1 ³/₄ cups)

1 Spray large ridged grill pan with nonstick spray and set over medium-high heat. Sprinkle pork with salt and pepper. Place in grill pan and cook until instant-read thermometer inserted into center of each chop registers 160°F for medium, 3–4 minutes on each side.

2 Meanwhile, to make salsa, place pineapple, shallot, fish sauce, brown sugar, cilantro, and pepper flakes in food processor and pulse 2–3 times, just until pineapple is coarsely chopped.

3 Heat rice according to package directions for microwave. Serve pork chops with rice and salsa.

PER SERVING (1 pork chop, scant ¹/₂ cup rice, + ¹/₄ cup salsa): 240 grams, 272 Cal, 7 g Total Fat, 2 g Sat Fat, 0 g Trans Fat, 66 mg Chol, 685 mg Sod, 28 g Carb, 6 g Sugar, 2 g Fib, 24 g Prot, 39 mg Calc.

F.Y.I.

Cooked brown rice is a convenient pantry staple to have on hand for quick weeknight meals. Look for it at the supermarket in plastic pouches near the dry rice.

Spiced Pork Chops with Scallion Couscous

- ▲ **4 (4-ounce) boneless center-cut loin pork chops, trimmed**
- **2 teaspoons ground coriander**
- **1 teaspoon ground cumin**
- **¾ teaspoon salt**
- **½ teaspoon black pepper**
- ▲ **1 cup reduced-sodium chicken broth**
- ▲ **1 cup whole wheat couscous**
- ▲ **2 scallions, thinly sliced**
- **4 lime wedges**

1 Spray large skillet with nonstick spray and set over medium-high heat. Sprinkle pork with coriander, cumin, ½ teaspoon of the salt, and ¼ teaspoon of the pepper. Place in skillet and cook until instant-read thermometer inserted into center of each chop registers 160°F for medium, 3–4 minutes on each side.

2 Meanwhile, bring broth to boil in medium saucepan. Add couscous, cover, and remove from heat. Let stand 5 minutes. Add scallions and remaining ¼ teaspoon salt and ¼ teaspoon pepper; fluff with fork. Serve pork chops with couscous and lime wedges.

PER SERVING (1 pork chop + ⅔ cup couscous): 220 grams, 264 Cal, 7 g Total Fat, 2 g Sat Fat, 0 g Trans Fat, 66 mg Chol, 501 mg Sod, 24 g Carb, 0 g Sugar, 4 g Fib, 27 g Prot, 42 mg Calc.

▲ *Healthy Extra*

Serve the pork chops and couscous with a side of steamed spinach.

Shop Smart, Work Smart

Make the most of the ingredients you buy and the time you spend in the kitchen with these tips:

■ **Keep Recipe-Ready Veggies on Hand.** Stock up on pre-cut vegetables such as carrots, mushrooms, bell peppers, and broccoli florets. You can use them throughout the week for stir-fries, soups, and salads or you can serve them with a dip for snacks. To save money, do the prep yourself and store the veggies in resealable plastic bags.

■ **Stock Up on Double-Duty Ingredients.** Keep a generous supply of canned pantry basics on hand (such as beans, diced tomatoes, and broths) that can be used in many different types of dishes. Beans can go into soups, salads, and dips; use diced tomatoes to make a sauce, a soup, or a casserole; and broths are indispensible for making soups and cooking grains.

■ **Cook Double the Amount.** If you know you'll have pasta and rice at least a couple of times each week, make more than you need so you'll have extra portions to use throughout the week.

■ **Make the Most of Down Time.** Use your time in the kitchen wisely. While you're waiting for the oven to preheat or the pasta water to boil, prep the other ingredients for dinner, make a salad, or wash small utensils.

■ **Be a Multitasker.** Get longer cooking items going first, then make quick-cooking side dishes at the same time. If you're having a baked entrée, get it in the oven, then focus on making a whole grain pasta side dish and a steamed vegetable to serve alongside.

■ **Plan Leftovers.** On the weekend, make at least one dish that you can serve leftover during the week. Slow-cooking stews or hearty roasts reheat beautifully and will be make a welcome dinner in mid-week.

Pork Pitas with Chutney Sauce

▲ **1 (1-pound) pork tenderloin, cut into 8 (¹/₂-inch) slices**

1 teaspoon smoked hot paprika

¹/₂ teaspoon salt

▲ **¹/₂ cup plain fat-free Greek yogurt**

2 tablespoons fruit chutney (such as fig or apple)

4 (6-inch) whole wheat pita breads, warmed

▲ **2 cups baby arugula**

1 Spray large ridged grill pan with nonstick spray and set over medium-high heat. Sprinkle pork with paprika and salt. Place in grill pan and cook until instant-read thermometer inserted into center of pork registers 160°F for medium, 3–4 minutes on each side.

2 Meanwhile, to make sauce, stir together yogurt and chutney in small bowl; set aside.

3 Halve pita breads; fill each half evenly with pork and arugula. Drizzle with sauce and serve at once.

Per Serving

PER SERVING *(2 filled pita halves): 135 grams, 240 Cal, 4 g Total Fat, 1 g Sat Fat, 0 g Trans Fat, 62 mg Chol, 527 mg Sod, 22 g Carb, 4 g Sugar, 3 g Fib, 28 g Prot, 66 mg Calc.*

▲ *Healthy Extra*

To give the sandwiches more crunch and extra sweetness, add some thin apple or pear slices along with the arugula.

*Rosemary Lamb Chops
with Balsamic Tomatoes*

Rosemary Lamb Chops with Balsamic Tomatoes

SERVES 4

▲ **4 (¼-pound) bone-in loin lamb chops, trimmed**

2 tablespoons chopped fresh rosemary

¾ teaspoon salt

½ teaspoon black pepper

▲ **2 cups cherry tomatoes**

▲ **2 scallions, thinly sliced**

2 tablespoons balsamic vinegar

▲ *Healthy Extra*

Serve the lamb and tomatoes with brown rice (⅔ cup cooked brown rice for each serving will increase the **PointsPlus** value by **3**).

1 Spray large nonstick skillet with nonstick spray and set over medium-high heat. Sprinkle lamb with rosemary, ½ teaspoon of the salt, and ¼ teaspoon of the pepper. Place in skillet and cook until instant-read thermometer inserted into center of each chop registers 145°F for medium-rare, 3–4 minutes on each side. Transfer lamb to plate and keep warm.

2 Add tomatoes and scallions to skillet and cook, stirring often, just until tomatoes are softened, about 2 minutes. Add vinegar and remaining ¼ teaspoon salt and ¼ teaspoon pepper and cook 30 seconds. Serve lamb with tomatoes.

3 PointsPlus value Per Serving

PER SERVING (1 lamb chop + ½ cup tomatoes): 195 grams, 107 Cal, 4 g Total Fat, 2 g Sat Fat, 0 g Trans Fat, 47 mg Chol, 466 mg Sod, 5 g Carb, 3 g Sugar, 1 g Fib, 13 g Prot, 28 mg Calc.

Pan-Seared Lamb Chops with Wilted Watercress

▲ **4 (¼-pound) bone-in loin lamb chops, trimmed**

½ teaspoon salt

¼ teaspoon black pepper

▲ **2 bunches watercress, trimmed**

2 garlic cloves, minced

1 tablespoon reduced-sodium soy sauce

1 tablespoon rice vinegar

1 teaspoon Asian (dark) sesame oil

▲ **1 (8.8-ounce) package cooked brown rice (about 1 ¾ cups)**

1 Spray large nonstick skillet with nonstick spray and set over medium-high heat. Sprinkle lamb with salt and pepper. Place in skillet and cook until instant-read thermometer inserted into center of each chop registers 145°F for medium-rare, 3–4 minutes on each side. Transfer lamb to plate and keep warm.

2 Add watercress, garlic, soy sauce, vinegar, and oil to skillet and cook, stirring constantly, until watercress is wilted, about 1 minute.

3 Heat rice according to package directions for microwave. Serve lamb with rice and watercress.

PER SERVING *(1 lamb chop, scant ½ cup rice, + ½ cup watercress): 230 grams, 199 Cal, 5 g Total Fat, 2 g Sat Fat, 0 g Trans Fat, 47 mg Chol, 471 mg Sod, 22 g Carb, 0 g Sugar, 2 g Fib, 16 g Prot, 89 mg Calc.*

F.Y.I.

To save time, **look for pre-washed watercress** in the produce section of the supermarket. You can use arugula or baby spinach instead of watercress in this recipe if you wish.

Chicken and Polenta with Zucchini-Tomato Sauce

SERVES 4

- ▲ **1 (16-ounce) tube refrigerated fat-free plain polenta, cut into 8 rounds**
- ▲ **4 (5-ounce) skinless boneless chicken breasts**
- **$1/2$ teaspoon salt**
- **$1/4$ teaspoon black pepper**
- ▲ **1 medium zucchini, diced**
- ▲ **1 (8-ounce) can no-salt-added tomato sauce**
- **2 tablespoons water**
- **Pinch saffron**

F.Y.I.

If you don't have saffron on hand, use 1 tablespoon chopped fresh basil or 1 teaspoon dried basil instead. The flavor won't be the same, but the dish will still be delicious.

1 Preheat broiler. Spray large baking sheet with nonstick spray. Arrange polenta in single layer on baking sheet. Broil polenta 4 inches from heat until lightly browned and heated through, 6–8 minutes.

2 Meanwhile, spray large nonstick skillet with nonstick spray and set over medium-high heat. Sprinkle chicken with salt and pepper. Place in skillet and cook, turning occasionally, until well browned and cooked through, about 8 minutes. Transfer to plate and keep warm.

3 Add zucchini to skillet and cook, stirring often, until just crisp-tender, about 2 minutes. Add tomato sauce, water, and saffron and cook just until heated through, about 1 minute.

4 Divide polenta evenly among 4 serving plates, top with chicken, and spoon sauce over chicken.

PER SERVING (1 chicken breast, 2 slices polenta, + $1/3$ cup sauce): 215 grams, 266 Cal, 4 g Total Fat, 1 g Sat Fat, 0 g Trans Fat, 78 mg Chol, 722 mg Sod, 24 g Carb, 5 g Sugar, 3 g Fib, 32 g Prot, 30 mg Calc.

Mustard Chicken with Black-Eyed Pea Salad

▲ **4 (5-ounce) skinless boneless chicken breasts**

3 tablespoons plus 1 teaspoon coarse-grained mustard

½ teaspoon salt

½ teaspoon black pepper

▲ **1 (15-ounce) can black-eyed peas, rinsed and drained**

▲ **1 cup frozen corn kernels, thawed**

▲ **⅓ cup chopped red onion**

¼ cup apple-cider vinegar

3 tablespoons chopped fresh flat-leaf parsley

1 Spray broiler rack with nonstick spray; preheat broiler.

2 Combine chicken, 3 tablespoons of the mustard, ¼ teaspoon of the salt, and ¼ teaspoon of the pepper in shallow dish. Turn chicken to coat. Place chicken on prepared broiler rack and broil 4 inches from heat, turning once, until chicken is cooked through, 4–5 minutes on each side.

3 Meanwhile, to make salad, stir together black-eyed peas, corn, onion, vinegar, parsley, and remaining 1 teaspoon mustard, ¼ teaspoon salt, and ¼ teaspoon pepper in medium bowl. Serve chicken with salad.

PER SERVING (1 chicken breast + ⅔ cup salad): 180 grams, 278 Cal, 5 g Total Fat, 1 g Sat Fat, 0 g Trans Fat, 78 mg Chol, 544 mg Sod, 25 g Carb, 1 g Sugar, 4 g Fib, 35 g Prot, 47 mg Calc.

▲ **Healthy Extra**

To add some healthful greens to this meal, serve the chicken and salad on a bed of leaf lettuce.

Mustard Chicken with Black-Eyed Pea Salad

Chili-Glazed Chicken with Cucumber-Mint Salad

▲ **4 (5-ounce) skinless boneless chicken breasts**

½ teaspoon salt

½ teaspoon black pepper

2 tablespoons Asian sweet chili sauce

2 tablespoons water

1 tablespoon rice vinegar

2 teaspoons Asian fish sauce

▲ **1 large English (seedless) cucumber, thinly sliced**

2 tablespoons chopped fresh mint

 ▲ **Healthy Extra**

Add 6 to 8 thinly sliced radishes to the cucumber mixture in step 3.

1 Spray large nonstick skillet with nonstick spray and set over medium-high heat. Sprinkle chicken with ¼ teaspoon of the salt and ¼ teaspoon of the pepper. Place in skillet and cook, turning occasionally, until well browned and cooked through, about 8 minutes. Transfer to plate and keep warm.

2 Meanwhile, stir together chili sauce, water, vinegar, and fish sauce in small bowl. Add chili sauce mixture to skillet and bring just to boil. Remove from heat.

3 Toss together cucumber, mint, and remaining ¼ teaspoon salt and ¼ teaspoon pepper. Divide cucumber mixture evenly among 4 serving plates. Top with chicken and drizzle evenly with chili sauce mixture.

PER SERVING (1 chicken breast, about ½ cup cucumber misture + 1 tablespoon sauce): 225 grams, 165 Cal, 4 g Total Fat, 1 g Sat Fat, 0 g Trans Fat, 78 mg Chol, 779 mg Sod, 2 g Carb, 1 g Sugar, 1 g Fib, 29 g Prot, 29 mg Calc.

Lemon Chicken with Arugula and Tomato Salad

SERVES 4

- ▲ **4 (5-ounce) skinless boneless chicken breasts**
- **³/₄ teaspoon salt**
- **¹/₂ teaspoon black pepper**
- **Grated zest and juice of 1 large lemon**
- ▲ **6 cups packed arugula**
- ▲ **1 cup cherry tomatoes, halved**
- **1 teaspoon olive oil**

1 Spray large nonstick skillet with nonstick spray and set over medium-high heat. Sprinkle chicken with ½ teaspoon of the salt, ¼ teaspoon of the pepper, and the lemon zest. Place in skillet and cook, turning occasionally, until well browned and cooked through, about 8 minutes.

2 Meanwhile, toss together arugula, tomatoes, lemon juice, oil, and remaining ¼ teaspoon salt and ¼ teaspoon pepper. Divide salad evenly among 4 serving plates. Top with chicken.

PER SERVING *(1 chicken breast + 2 ½ cups salad): 150 grams, 183 Cal, 5 g Total Fat, 1 g Sat Fat, 0 g Trans Fat, 78 mg Chol, 515 mg Sod, 4 g Carb, 2 g Sugar, 1 g Fib, 30 g Prot, 72 mg Calc.*

▲ Healthy Extra

Add a satisfying whole grain side dish to this meal by serving it with bulgur. A half-cup of cooked bulgur per serving will increase the **PointsPlus** value by **2**.

Chicken and Broccoli with
Black Bean Sauce

Chicken and Broccoli with Black Bean Sauce

SERVES 4

▲ ¾ *pound chicken tenders, cut lengthwise into ¼-inch slices*

▲ *4 cups small broccoli florets*

▲ *1 red bell pepper, thinly sliced*

¼ cup plus 2 tablespoons water

2 tablespoons black bean sauce

1 teaspoon sugar

▲ *1 (8.8-ounce) package cooked brown rice (about 1 ¾ cups)*

1 Spray large wok or skillet with nonstick spray and set over medium-high heat. Add chicken and stir-fry until browned and just cooked through, 2–3 minutes. Transfer to plate.

2 Add broccoli, bell pepper, and ¼ cup of the water to wok; stir-fry until vegetables are crisp-tender, about 3 minutes. Add chicken, black bean sauce, sugar, and remaining 2 tablespoons water; stir-fry 1 minute.

3 Heat rice according to package directions for microwave. Serve chicken and vegetables with rice.

PER SERVING *(1 cup chicken and vegetables + scant ½ cup rice): 225 grams, 228 Cal, 4 g Total Fat, 1 g Sat Fat, 0 g Trans Fat, 47 mg Chol, 117 mg Sod, 27 g Carb, 2 g Sugar, 4 g Fib, 22 g Prot, 56 mg Calc.*

▲ *Healthy Extra*

Make this stir-fry even more filling and colorful by adding a thinly sliced green or yellow bell pepper with the broccoli in step 2.

Chicken and Noodles with Black and Red Pepper

SERVES 4

▲ *1 (9-ounce) package refrigerated whole wheat linguine*

▲ *¹⁄₂ pound chicken tenders, cut into ¹⁄₄-inch strips*

▲ *2 baby bok choy, cut into 1-inch pieces*

▲ *2 scallions, thinly sliced*

▲ *¹⁄₂ cup shredded carrot*

1 garlic clove, minced

3 tablespoons reduced-sodium soy sauce

1 teaspoon sugar

¹⁄₂ teaspoon black pepper

¹⁄₄ teaspoon red pepper flakes

1 Cook linguine according to package directions, omitting salt if desired. Drain and keep warm.

2 Meanwhile, spray large wok or skillet with nonstick spray and set over medium-high heat. Add chicken and stir-fry until browned and just cooked through, 2–3 minutes; transfer to plate.

3 Add bok choy, scallions, carrot, and garlic to wok; stir-fry until vegetables are softened, about 2 minutes. Add chicken, soy sauce, sugar, black pepper, pepper flakes, and pasta and stir-fry until heated through, about 1 minute.

PER SERVING *(1 ¹⁄₄ cups): 175 grams, 167 Cal, 2 g Total Fat, 0 g Sat Fat, 0 g Trans Fat, 31 mg Chol, 463 mg Sod, 22 g Carb, 3 g Sugar, 4 g Fib, 16 g Prot, 30 mg Calc.*

▲ *Healthy Extra*

Stir 2 cups shredded cucumbers into the dish just before serving.

Poppy Seed Chicken and Clementine Salad

SERVES 4

2 tablespoons red-wine vinegar

1 tablespoon honey

1 tablespoon water

$1/2$ small shallot, sliced

1 teaspoon Dijon mustard

1 teaspoon extra-virgin olive oil

$1/2$ teaspoon poppy seeds

Pinch salt

Pinch black pepper

▲ 6 cups packed mixed baby greens

▲ 2 cups chopped cooked chicken breast

▲ 4 clementines, peeled and separated into segments

1 To make dressing, place vinegar, honey, water, shallot, mustard, oil, poppy seeds, salt, and pepper in mini food processor; process until shallot is finely chopped and dressing is well blended.

2 Combine greens, chicken, and clementines in large bowl; drizzle with dressing and toss to coat.

PER SERVING (2 $1/2$ cups): 195 grams, 199 Cal, 4 g Total Fat, 1 g Sat Fat, 0 g Trans Fat, 60 mg Chol, 150 mg Sod, 18 g Carb, 13 g Sugar, 3 g Fib, 24 g Prot, 41 mg Calc.

To make this salad even more healthful and filling, toss in 1 cup of red or green seedless grapes.

Greek Chicken with Peppers and Pasta

SERVES 4

- ▲ **8 ounces whole wheat penne or fusilli**

  ½ teaspoon salt

- ▲ **1 sweet onion, halved lengthwise and sliced**

- ▲ **2 cups chopped cooked chicken breast**

- ▲ **1 cup sliced pepperoncini, drained**

- ▲ **½ cup chopped roasted red bell peppers (not oil-packed)**

  1 teaspoon extra-virgin olive oil

  ¼ cup crumbled reduced-fat feta cheese

  2 tablespoons chopped fresh oregano

1 Place pasta and salt in large skillet; add cold water to cover. Bring to boil over high heat; cook, uncovered, stirring occasionally, until pasta is al dente, about 8 minutes. Drain.

2 Meanwhile, spray large skillet with nonstick spray and set over medium-high heat. Add onion and cook, stirring occasionally, until softened, about 3 minutes. Add chicken, pepperoncini, and roasted peppers; cook, stirring often, until heated through, about 2 minutes. Add pasta and oil and toss until combined. Divide pasta mixture evenly among 4 serving plates; sprinkle evenly with feta and oregano.

Per Serving

PER SERVING *(2 cups): 260 grams, 312 Cal, 5 g Total Fat, 1 g Sat Fat, 0 g Trans Fat, 17 mg Chol, 714 mg Sod, 52 g Carb, 7 g Sugar, 7 g Fib, 15 g Prot, 82 mg Calc.*

F.Y.I.

In several recipes in this chapter, including this one, **pasta is cooked in a small amount of water** instead of the usual large pot of boiling water. It's a time-saving method that results in delicious pasta in a hurry.

Greek Chicken with Peppers and Pasta

Kielbasa with Pasta, Chickpeas, and Spinach

Kielbasa with Pasta, Chickpeas, and Spinach

SERVES 4

▲ **8 ounces whole wheat penne or fusilli**

½ teaspoon salt

6 ounces turkey kielbasa, cut into ¼-inch slices

▲ **4 cups baby spinach**

▲ **1 cup canned chickpeas, rinsed and drained**

▲ **3 scallions, thinly sliced**

1 garlic clove, minced

Pinch red pepper flakes

1 teaspoon extra-virgin olive oil

2 tablespoons grated Pecorino Romano or Parmesan cheese

1 Place pasta and salt in large skillet; add cold water to cover. Bring to boil over high heat; cook, uncovered, stirring occasionally, until pasta is al dente, about 8 minutes. Drain.

2 Meanwhile, spray large nonstick skillet with nonstick spray and set over medium-high heat. Add kielbasa and cook, stirring occasionally, until lightly browned, about 2 minutes. Add spinach, chickpeas, scallions, garlic, and pepper flakes and cook, stirring often, until spinach is wilted, about 2 minutes. Add pasta and oil and toss to combine. Divide pasta mixture evenly among 4 serving plates; sprinkle evenly with cheese.

PER SERVING (1 ½ cups pasta mixture + ½ tablespoon cheese): 190 grams, 383 Cal, 8 g Total Fat, 2 g Sat Fat, 0 g Trans Fat, 29 mg Chol, 774 mg Sod, 59 g Carb, 4 g Sugar, 9 g Fib, 18 g Prot, 100 mg Calc.

Turkey and Arugula with Lemon-Balsamic Sauce

SERVES 4

▲ **1 pound turkey breast tenderloin, cut into ¹/₂-inch slices**

¹/₂ teaspoon salt

¹/₄ teaspoon black pepper

¹/₄ cup balsamic vinegar

¹/₄ cup water

2 tablespoons lemon juice

1 tablespoon brown sugar

▲ **4 cups packed baby arugula**

1 Spray large nonstick skillet with nonstick spray and set over medium-high heat. Sprinkle turkey with salt and pepper. Place in skillet and cook, turning once, until well browned and cooked through, 6–8 minutes. Transfer to plate and keep warm.

2 Meanwhile, to make sauce, stir together vinegar, water, lemon juice, and brown sugar. Add to skillet and bring to boil; cook, stirring often, until mixture is reduced by half, about 2 minutes.

3 Divide arugula evenly among 4 serving plates; top evenly with turkey and drizzle with sauce.

4 PointsPlus® value
Per Serving

PER SERVING (1 plate): 145 grams, 156 Cal, 2 g Total Fat, 0 g Sat Fat, 0 g Trans Fat, 45 mg Chol, 366 mg Sod, 8 g Carb, 6 g Sugar, 0 g Fib, 29 g Prot, 41 mg Calc.

▲ **Healthy Extra**

Add a sliced cucumber and 1 cup of grape tomatoes to the arugula to add more bulk and color to this dish.

Pan-Roasted Salmon with Lentils and Feta

SERVES 4

4 (6-ounce) salmon fillets

¾ teaspoon salt

½ teaspoon black pepper

▲ 2 scallions, thinly sliced

▲ 1 medium zucchini, diced

▲ 2 cups precooked green (French) lentils

2 tablespoons crumbled reduced-fat feta cheese

F.Y.I.

Precooked lentils are available in vacuum-sealed packages in many supermarkets. If you can't find them, substitute a 15 ½ ounce can navy beans, rinsed and drained in this recipe.

---

1 Spray large nonstick skillet with nonstick spray and set over medium-high heat. Sprinkle salmon with ½ teaspoon of the salt and ¼ teaspoon of the pepper. Place in skillet and cook until lightly browned and just opaque in center, 4–5 minutes on each side. Transfer to plate and keep warm.

2 Spray same skillet with nonstick spray and set over medium-high heat. Add scallions and zucchini and cook, stirring often, until zucchini is crisp-tender, about 3 minutes. Add lentils and remaining ¼ teaspoon salt and ¼ teaspoon pepper; cook, stirring often, until heated through, about 2 minutes. Divide lentil mixture evenly among 4 serving plates and top with salmon. Sprinkle evenly with feta.

Per Serving

PER SERVING *(1 fish fillet, ¾ cup lentil mixture, + ½ tablespoon cheese): 250 grams, 413 Cal, 14 g Total Fat, 2 g Sat Fat, 0 g Trans Fat, 109 mg Chol, 588 mg Sod, 22 g Carb, 3 g Sugar, 9 g Fib, 49 g Prot, 68 mg Calc.*

Hoisin-Glazed Tilapia with Soba Noodles

▲ **6 ounces soba noodles**

▲ **½ English (seedless) cucumber, coarsely shredded**

2 tablespoons reduced-sodium soy sauce

▲ **4 (5-ounce) tilapia fillets**

½ teaspoon salt

¼ teaspoon black pepper

1 tablespoon hoisin sauce

1 teaspoon Asian red chili sauce

F.Y.I.

Asian red chili sauce, sometimes called sambal oelek or Sriracha, is a spicy blend of peppers, vinegar, and sometimes sugar. **Brands vary in how spicy they are**, so always add with caution.

1 Spray broiler rack with nonstick spray; preheat broiler.

2 Cook noodles according to package directions, omitting salt if desired. Drain and rinse under cold running water; drain again. Transfer noodles to medium bowl; add cucumber and soy sauce and toss to coat.

3 Meanwhile, sprinkle tilapia with salt and pepper and place on prepared broiler rack. Broil 5 minutes. Stir together hoisin sauce and chili sauce in small dish. Brush tilapia with hoisin mixture and broil until fish is just opaque in center, about 1 minute longer. Serve fish with noodles.

8 PointsPlus® value ™ Per Serving

PER SERVING *(1 fish fillet + 1 cup noodles): 230 grams, 303 Cal, 4 g Total Fat, 1 g Sat Fat, 0 g Trans Fat, 61 mg Chol, 685 mg Sod, 35 g Carb, 3 g Sugar, 6 g Fib, 35 g Prot, 43 mg Calc.*

Warm Tuna, Butter Bean, and Pasta Salad

▲ **6 ounces whole wheat rotini or penne**

¾ teaspoon salt

▲ **1 (15 ½-ounce) can butter beans, rinsed and drained**

▲ **1 (6-ounce) can water-packed light tuna, drained and flaked**

▲ **2 cups chopped arugula**

▲ **¼ cup chopped red onion**

Grated zest and juice of 1 lemon

1 teaspoon extra-virgin olive oil

¼ teaspoon black pepper

Pinch cayenne

1 Place pasta and salt in large skillet; add cold water to cover. Bring to boil over high heat; cook, uncovered, stirring occasionally, until pasta is al dente, about 8 minutes. Drain.

2 Meanwhile, combine remaining ingredients in large bowl; add pasta and toss to coat.

PER SERVING (1 ¾ cups): 215 grams, 229 Cal, 3 g Total Fat, 0 g Sat Fat, 0 g Trans Fat, 13 mg Chol, 591 mg Sod, 35 g Carb, 3 g Sugar, 4 g Fib, 17 g Prot, 42 mg Calc.

F.Y.I.

Butter beans are a large white variety of lima beans. If you prefer, you can use canned navy beans or cannellini (white kidney) beans in this recipe instead.

Quick Clam and Roasted Pepper Paella

2 teaspoons olive oil

▲ *1 medium red onion, chopped*

1 garlic clove, minced

2 tablespoons dry sherry

1 teaspoon smoked paprika

▲ *2 cups instant brown rice*

▲ *1 ½ cups reduced-sodium chicken broth*

▲ *1 pound manila or other small clams, cleaned*

▲ *⅓ cup roasted red bell peppers, drained and chopped (not oil-packed)*

½ teaspoon salt

▲ *1 cup frozen green peas*

1 Heat oil in large nonstick skillet over medium-high heat. Add onion and garlic; cook, stirring often, until softened, 3 minutes. Add sherry and paprika and cook, stirring constantly, until fragrant, 30 seconds.

2 Add rice, broth, clams, roasted peppers, and salt to skillet and bring to boil. Reduce heat and simmer, covered, until clams open, about 5 minutes. Stir in peas; remove from heat and let stand, covered, 5 minutes longer. Fluff rice with fork. Discard any clams that do not open.

PER SERVING (1 ½ cups): 255 grams, 476 Cal, 6 g Total Fat, 1 g Sat Fat, 0 g Trans Fat, 11 mg Chol, 500 mg Sod, 88 g Carb, 4 g Sugar, 9 g Fib, 16 g Prot, 75 mg Calc.

Healthy Extra

Add 2 cups baby spinach when you stir in the peas in step 2.

Spicy Thai Crab Rolls with Basil

SERVES 4

- ▲ **12 ounces fresh or canned crabmeat, picked over for pieces of shell**

- **2 tablespoons reduced-fat mayonnaise**

- **1 teaspoon grated lime zest**

- **1 tablespoon lime juice**

- **1 teaspoon Asian fish sauce**

- **⅛ teaspoon chili-garlic sauce or hot pepper sauce**

- **4 whole wheat hot dog buns, split and toasted**

- ▲ **1 (4-ounce) package radish sprouts**

- **12 fresh small basil leaves**

1 Stir together crabmeat, mayonnaise, lime zest and juice, fish sauce, and chili-garlic sauce in medium bowl.

2 Fill buns evenly with crabmeat mixture; top evenly with radish sprouts and basil.

PER SERVING *(1 roll): 140 grams, 221 Cal, 5 g Total Fat, 1 g Sat Fat, 0 g Trans Fat, 60 mg Chol, 702 mg Sod, 24 g Carb, 4 g Sugar, 3 g Fib, 23 g Prot, 125 mg Calc.*

▲ Healthy Extra

To make an Asian-inspired slaw, toss together 4 cups thinly sliced cabbage, 4 shredded radishes, 1 shredded carrot, 2 tablespoons reduced-sodium soy sauce, and 1 tablespoon lime juice in a large bowl.

Halibut and Asparagus with Tomato Sauce

SERVES 4

- ▲ **4 (5-ounce) halibut fillets**

  ³/₄ teaspoon salt

  ¹/₂ teaspoon black pepper

- ▲ **1 pound thin asparagus, trimmed**

  2 teaspoons olive oil

  1 garlic clove, minced

  1 teaspoon ground coriander

- ▲ **1 (14 ¹/₂-ounce) can diced tomatoes**

  2 tablespoons chopped fresh parsley

▲ Healthy Extra

Serve this dish with whole wheat couscous to soak up the flavorful tomato sauce (⅔ cup cooked whole wheat couscous per serving will increase the **PointsPlus** value by **3**.)

1 Spray broiler rack with nonstick spray; preheat broiler.

2 Sprinkle halibut with ¹/₂ teaspoon of the salt and ¹/₄ teaspoon of the pepper. Place on prepared broiler rack. Place asparagus on broiler rack; spray lightly with nonstick spray. Sprinkle with remaining ¹/₄ teaspoon salt and ¹/₄ teaspoon pepper; toss to coat. Broil 5 minutes. Turn asparagus; broil until fish is just opaque in center and asparagus is crisp-tender, 3–4 minutes longer.

3 Meanwhile, heat oil in large nonstick skillet over medium-high heat. Add garlic and coriander and cook, stirring constantly, until fragrant, 30 seconds. Add tomatoes and bring to boil. Cook, stirring occasionally, until sauce is slightly thickened, about 3 minutes. Divide halibut and asparagus evenly among 4 serving plates; spoon sauce evenly over halibut. Sprinkle with parsley.

5 PointsPlus value
Per Serving

PER SERVING *(1 fish fillet, about 10 asparagus spears, + ¹/₃ cup sauce): 210 grams, 220 Cal, 6 g Total Fat, 1 g Sat Fat, 0 g Trans Fat, 44 mg Chol, 741 mg Sod, 10 g Carb, 5 g Sugar, 3 g Fib, 32 g Prot, 110 mg Calc.*

*Halibut and Asparagus
with Tomato Sauce*

Hot-and-Sour Tofu and Vegetable Soup

SERVES 4

▲ 3 cups reduced-sodium vegetable broth

3 cups water

▲ 4 cups coleslaw mix

▲ 1 cup sliced fresh mushrooms

3 tablespoons white vinegar

2 tablespoons minced peeled fresh ginger

1 teaspoon black pepper

▲ 14 ounces reduced-fat firm tofu, cut into ½-inch cubes

3 tablespoons reduced-sodium soy sauce

1 tablespoon cornstarch

2 teaspoons Asian (dark) sesame oil

¼ teaspoon salt

▲ 2 scallions, thinly sliced (optional)

1 Bring broth, water, coleslaw mix, mushrooms, vinegar, ginger, and pepper to boil in large saucepan over high heat. Reduce heat and simmer, covered, 5 minutes. Stir in tofu and cook until heated through, 1 minute.

2 Stir together soy sauce and cornstarch in small bowl; stir into soup. Simmer until soup is slightly thickened, about 1 minute. Stir in oil and salt. Ladle soup evenly into 4 serving bowls; sprinkle with scallions, if using.

PER SERVING *(about 2 cups): 390 grams, 99 Cal, 3 g Total Fat, 0 g Sat Fat, 0 g Trans Fat, 0 mg Chol, 474 mg Sod, 10 g Carb, 2 g Sugar, 3 g Fib, 7 g Prot, 296 mg Calc.*

▲ Healthy Extra

To add more protein to this soup, slowly drizzle 2 lightly beaten large eggs into the soup after you add the soy sauce mixture. Simmer about 1 minute. The per-serving **PointsPlus** value will increase by **1**.

Tofu-Noodle Vegetable Wraps

4 ounces cellophane noodles (bean thread vermicelli)

¼ cup reduced-sodium soy sauce

1 tablespoon lime juice

1 garlic clove, minced

▲ ½ jalapeño pepper, seeded and minced

▲ 4 ounces baked tofu, cut into ½-inch cubes

▲ 1 large carrot, shredded

▲ ¾ cup thinly sliced English (seedless) cucumber

▲ ¾ cup thinly sliced red bell pepper

¼ cup chopped fresh mint

▲ 8 Bibb or green leaf lettuce leaves (optional)

1 Place noodles in large bowl. Add boiling water to cover. Let stand until softened, about 5 minutes. Drain and coarsely chop noodles.

2 Meanwhile, stir together soy sauce, lime juice, garlic, and jalapeño in small bowl.

3 Transfer noodles to medium bowl. Add tofu, carrot, cucumber, bell pepper, and mint; drizzle with 2 tablespoons of the soy sauce mixture and toss to combine.

4 Arrange 2 lettuce leaves on each of 4 serving plates. Fill each lettuce leaf with about ½ cup of the noodle mixture. Drizzle evenly with remaining soy sauce mixture.

4 PointsPlus value ™ Per Serving

PER SERVING (2 wraps): 180 grams, 158 Cal, 2 g Total Fat, 0 g Sat Fat, 0 g Trans Fat, 0 mg Chol, 552 mg Sod, 32 g Carb, 3 g Sugar, 2 g Fib, 4 g Prot, 86 mg Calc.

Beans, Greens, and
Pasta Soup

Beans, Greens, and Pasta Soup

SERVES 4

2 teaspoons olive oil

1 garlic clove, minced

▲ **2 cups packed chopped escarole**

▲ **2 cups reduced-sodium vegetable broth**

2 cups water

¹/₂ teaspoon dried oregano

¹/₄ teaspoon salt

¹/₈ teaspoon red pepper flakes

▲ **1 (15 ¹/₂-ounce) can Roman beans or cannellini (white kidney) beans, rinsed and drained**

▲ **1 (9-ounce) package refrigerated whole wheat linguine**

4 tablespoons grated Parmesan cheese

1 Heat oil in large saucepan over medium-high heat. Add garlic and cook, stirring constantly, until fragrant, 30 seconds. Add escarole and cook, stirring often, until wilted, about 1 minute. Add broth, water, oregano, salt, and pepper flakes; cover and bring to boil over high heat.

2 Stir beans and linguine into saucepan; return to boil. Reduce heat and simmer, uncovered, until pasta is tender, 2–3 minutes.

3 Ladle soup evenly into 4 serving bowls and sprinkle evenly with Parmesan.

PER SERVING *(about 2 cups soup + 1 tablespoon cheese): 399 grams, 227 Cal, 4 g Total Fat, 1 g Sat Fat, 0 g Trans Fat, 4 mg Chol, 591 mg Sod, 37 g Carb, 3 g Sugar, 9 g Fib, 12 g Prot, 146 mg Calc.*

▲ *Healthy Extra*

Add 2 chopped plum tomatoes when you add the beans in step 2.

Corn and Black Bean Enchilada Casserole

SERVES 4

1 teaspoon olive oil

▲ *1 small onion, finely chopped*

1 garlic clove, minced

▲ *1 (15-ounce) can no-salt-added tomato sauce*

1 tablespoon chili powder

▲ *1 (15 ½-ounce) can reduced-sodium black beans, rinsed and drained*

▲ *1 cup fresh or thawed frozen corn kernels*

4 (8-inch) whole wheat tortillas, each cut into 6 wedges

⅓ cup shredded low-fat Mexican cheese blend

1 Spray 7 x 11-inch baking dish with nonstick spray.

2 To make sauce, heat oil in medium nonstick skillet over medium heat. Add onion and garlic and cook, stirring occasionally, until onion is softened, about 3 minutes. Add tomato sauce and chili powder; bring to boil. Reduce heat and simmer 2 minutes.

3 Meanwhile, stir together beans and corn in medium bowl. Arrange 8 of the tortilla wedges in overlapping layer in bottom of prepared baking dish. Spoon one-third of the sauce on top; top with half of the bean mixture. Repeat layering with 8 of the remaining tortilla wedges, half of the remaining sauce, and the remaining bean mixture. Top with remaining 8 tortilla wedges; spread with remaining sauce. Sprinkle with cheese blend.

4 Microwave casserole on High until cheese melts and sauce is bubbling, about 5 minutes.

PER SERVING *(1 cup): 220 grams, 335 Cal, 7 g Total Fat, 1 g Sat Fat, 0 g Trans Fat, 5 mg Chol, 507 mg Sod, 57 g Carb, 8 g Sugar, 10 g Fib, 14 g Prot, 194 mg Calc.*

▲ *Healthy Extra*

To make a Tex-Mex salad, combine 8 cups lettuce, 2 cups halved cherry tomatoes, and 1 sliced cucumber in a large bowl and toss with a squeeze of lime juice, a pinch of ground cumin, and salt and pepper to taste.

Three-Cheese and Tomato Pizzas

SERVES 4

4 (6-inch) whole wheat pocketless pita breads

¹/₂ cup crumbled goat cheese

¹/₂ cup shredded part-skim mozzarella cheese

▲ **1 cup grape tomatoes, halved**

¹/₄ cup grated Parmesan cheese

4 teaspoons chopped fresh oregano

1 Preheat broiler.

2 Arrange pita breads on baking sheet. Broil 4 inches from heat until heated through, about 1 minute on each side.

3 Top pita breads evenly with goat cheese and mozzarella. Arrange tomatoes evenly on top; sprinkle with Parmesan. Broil until cheese is melted, 2–3 minutes. Sprinkle with oregano.

PER SERVING *(1 pizza): 114 grams, 280 Cal, 9 g Total Fat, 5 g Sat Fat, 0 g Trans Fat, 19 mg Chol, 546 mg Sod, 38 g Carb, 2 g Sugar, 5 g Fib, 15 g Prot, 198 mg Calc.*

15 MIN

bonus

No time? No problem! You can make these creative breakfasts, lunches, sides, snacks, and sweets in 15 minutes flat. A handful of bold ingredients put together in brilliant ways means you are out of the kitchen fast.

Breakfast Egg Cup with Feta and Chives

SERVES 1

- ▲ *1 large egg*
- ▲ *1 large egg white*
- *2 tablespoons water*
- *1 teaspoon minced fresh chives*
- *1 tablespoon crumbled feta or goat cheese*

1 Spray 8-ounce microwavable coffee mug with nonstick spray. Add egg, egg white, water, and ½ teaspoon of the chives and mix with fork until blended.

2 Microwave on High 30 seconds; stir. Microwave until eggs are almost set, 10–15 seconds longer. Top with cheese and remaining ½ teaspoon chives. Serve at once.

PER SERVING *(1 egg cup): 126 grams, 116 Cal, 7 g Total Fat, 3 g Sat Fat, 0 g Trans Fat, 223 mg Chol, 226 mg Sod, 2 g Carb, 1 g Sugar, 0 g Fib, 11 g Prot, 70 mg Calc.*

Fruited Breakfast Couscous

SERVES 4

- *1 cup low-fat (1%) milk*
- *2 (3-inch-long) strips orange zest, removed with vegetable peeler*
- *⅛ teaspoon ground ginger*
- *Pinch salt*
- ▲ *⅔ cup whole wheat couscous*
- *½ cup tropical dried fruit bits*

1 Combine milk, orange zest, ginger, and salt in medium saucepan. Bring just to simmer over medium-high heat.

2 Add couscous and fruit bits to saucepan, cover, and remove from heat. Let stand 5 minutes. Fluff with fork; discard orange zest.

3 Divide couscous evenly among 4 serving bowls and serve at once.

PER SERVING *(⅓ cup): 93 grams, 149 Cal, 1 g Total Fat, 1 g Sat Fat, 0 g Trans Fat, 3 mg Chol, 80 mg Sod, 30 g Carb, 14 g Sugar, 3 g Fib, 5 g Prot, 79 mg Calc.*

Muesli with Apricots and Almonds

2 cups old-fashioned oats

¾ cup dried apricot halves, diced

¼ cup toasted wheat germ

¼ cup instant nonfat dry milk

¼ cup sliced almonds

¼ cup roasted unsalted sunflower seeds

Stir together all ingredients in large bowl. Store in airtight container up to 2 weeks.

PER SERVING (generous ½ cup): 72 grams, 222 Cal, 7 g Total Fat, 1 g Sat Fat, 0 g Trans Fat, 0 mg Chol, 18 mg Sod, 34 g Carb, 12 g Sugar, 6 g Fib, 8 g Prot, 61 mg Calc.

F.Y.I.

Muesli is traditionally served with milk, but you can also serve it with yogurt. Stir the milk or yogurt into the muesli and eat it right away, or **let it stand to soften, anywhere from 2 to 30 minutes.**

Tex-Mex Nacho Scramble

SERVES 4 **2**

1 teaspoon unsalted butter

▲ 2 scallions, thinly sliced

▲ 4 large egg whites

▲ 2 large eggs

2 tablespoons water

¼ teaspoon chipotle chile powder

¼ cup shredded reduced-fat Monterey Jack cheese

1 cup coarsely broken baked tortilla chips

▲ 2 tablespoons fat-free chunky, fresh salsa

2 tablespoons chopped fresh cilantro (optional)

1 Melt butter in medium nonstick skillet over medium heat. Add scallions and cook, stirring often, until softened, 2 minutes.

2 Meanwhile, lightly beat egg whites, eggs, water, and chile powder in medium bowl. Add egg mixture to skillet and cook, stirring, until scrambled, about 3 minutes. Remove from heat; stir in Monterey Jack.

3 Divide chips evenly among 2 serving plates; top evenly with egg mixture and salsa. Sprinkle with cilantro, if using.

PER SERVING *(1 plate): 163 grams, 316 Cal, 14 g Total Fat, 5 g Sat Fat, 0 g Trans Fat, 228 mg Chol, 670 mg Sod, 27 g Carb, 2 g Sugar, 2 g Fib, 20 g Prot, 287 mg Calc.*

▲ *Healthy Extra*

Cook ½ cup thinly sliced red or green bell pepper with the scallions in step 1.

*Tex-Mex Nacho
Scramble*

Yogurt-Topped Microwave-Baked Apples

SERVES 2

- ▲ **2 Gala apples, halved and cored**
- **2 teaspoons unsalted butter**
- **2 tablespoons mixed dried fruit bits**
- **2 teaspoons water**
- **1/2 teaspoon sugar**
- **1/8 teaspoon ground cinnamon**
- ▲ **4 tablespoons plain fat-free Greek yogurt**

1 Place apples, cut side up, in 9-inch pie plate. Dot apples with butter; sprinkle evenly with fruit bits, water, sugar, and cinnamon.

2 Cover pie plate with wax paper and microwave on High until apples are very tender, about 5 minutes. Let stand, covered, 2 minutes.

3 Transfer 2 apple halves to each of 2 serving bowls; spoon cooking juices over apples. Top evenly with yogurt and serve at once.

PER SERVING *(1 apple + 2 tablespoons yogurt): 268 grams, 176 Cal, 4 g Total Fat, 2 g Sat Fat, 0 g Trans Fat, 10 mg Chol, 27 mg Sod, 34 g Carb, 27 g Sugar, 5 g Fib, 3 g Prot, 38 mg Calc.*

Berry-Cereal Parfaits with Maple Yogurt

SERVES 2

- ▲ **1 cup plain fat-free Greek yogurt**
- **2 teaspoons maple syrup**
- **3/4 cup 7–whole grain puffed cereal**
- ▲ **3/4 cup mixed fresh berries (such as blueberries and sliced strawberries)**

1 Stir together yogurt and maple syrup in small bowl.

2 Alternately layer half of the yogurt mixture, cereal, and berries in each of 2 parfait glasses. Repeat layering and serve at once.

PER SERVING *(1 parfait): 133 grams, 65 Cal, 0 g Total Fat, 0 g Sat Fat, 0 g Trans Fat, 0 mg Chol, 22 mg Sod, 10 g Carb, 6 g Sugar, 1 g Fib, 6 g Prot, 45 mg Calc.*

The Streamlined Pantry

If your pantry is organized, you'll spend less time looking for ingredients and more time cooking—which means you'll get out of the kitchen more quickly. Minimize your kitchen duty with these tips:

■ **Keep Favorites Close By.** Store foods you use most often in a location where you can easily grab them. If it's pasta night at your house at least twice a week, then store pastas at the front of the shelf. Place the herbs and spices you use most often where they are easy to access without looking though dozens of jars. To make the hunt even easier, store foods in clear plastic containers so there's no time spent guessing what's inside.

■ **Seldom Used Should Be Seldom Seen.** Consider a separate shelf for items you want to keep, but rarely use. If you store cake decorations, specialty condiments, and exotic vinegars on the top shelf of a cupboard, it frees up space for canned tomatoes, rice, and olive oil that you use several times a week.

■ **Divide and Conquer.** Use cabinet and drawer dividers and bins to keep similar items together. If all your oils are in a single row, grains are all inside a plastic bin, and spices are inside a storage box, you'll never have to search for anything. Having all of the same items in one place makes it easy to create a shopping list, too.

■ **Regroup Repeatedly.** Once a month, take 15 minutes to go through your pantry and re-organize foods that are stored on the wrong shelf and discard any items that are past their expiration date. Use this opportunity to remind yourself to incorporate healthful new foods into weeknight meals. Put the quinoa, curry paste, and soba noodles front and center so you'll remember to cook with them.

■ **Buy in Bulk—If You've Got the Space.** A case of canned tomatoes that takes up most of your pantry space is no bargain. If you have a large panty, though, bulk shopping is a money-saving idea.

Chicken and Couscous Salad with Dried Cherries

SERVES 4

▲ **1 ¼ cups reduced-sodium chicken broth**

¾ teaspoon ground coriander

½ teaspoon salt

▲ **1 cup whole wheat couscous**

▲ **1 ¼ cups shredded cooked skinless chicken breast**

½ cup finely chopped dried sour cherries

2 tablespoons shelled pistachios

2 tablespoons seasoned rice vinegar

1 tablespoon olive oil

¼ teaspoon black pepper

1 Combine broth, coriander, and ¼ teaspoon of the salt in medium saucepan; bring to boil. Add couscous, cover, and remove from heat. Let stand 5 minutes.

2 Meanwhile, combine chicken, cherries, pistachios, vinegar, oil, remaining ¼ teaspoon salt, and the pepper in large bowl. Add couscous and toss to combine.

PER SERVING *(scant 1 ½ cups): 170 grams, 304 Cal, 8 g Total Fat, 1 g Sat Fat, 0 g Trans Fat, 37 mg Chol, 495 mg Sod, 39 g Carb, 10 g Sugar, 5 g Fib, 21 g Prot, 25 mg Calc.*

▲ *Healthy Extra*

Add a shredded carrot and 2 thinly sliced scallions to the broth mixture in step 1 before you add the couscous.

Thai-Style Chicken and Mushroom Soup

SERVES 4

- ▲ **1 (32-ounce) carton reduced-sodium chicken broth**

- ▲ **1 (15-ounce) can straw mushrooms, rinsed and drained**

  2 teaspoons Thai green curry paste

  Pinch salt

- ▲ **1 (5-ounce) skinless boneless chicken breast, thinly sliced**

  ¹⁄₂ cup fresh cilantro leaves

  2 tablespoons lime juice

1 Combine broth, mushrooms, curry paste, and salt in large saucepan; bring to boil over medium-high heat.

2 Add chicken and cook, stirring often, until cooked through, about 2 minutes. Remove saucepan from heat and stir in ¹⁄₄ cup of the cilantro and the lime juice.

3 Divide soup evenly among 4 serving bowls and sprinkle evenly with remaining ¹⁄₄ cup cilantro.

PER SERVING (1 ¹⁄₄ cups): 225 grams, 112 Cal, 3 g Total Fat, 1 g Sat Fat, 0 g Trans Fat, 20 mg Chol, 613 mg Sod, 8 g Carb, 0 g Sugar, 3 g Fib, 16 g Prot, 24 mg Calc.

▲ Healthy Extra

To make the soup more filling, add 1 cup cooked whole wheat capellini when you add the chicken. The per-serving **PointsPlus** value will increase by **1**.

*Turkey Sausage and
Cranberry Sandwiches*

Turkey Sausage and Cranberry Sandwiches

SERVES 4

4 (4-ounce) Italian turkey sausage links

2 (4-ounce) whole grain hero rolls, halved, split and toasted

½ cup whole-berry cranberry sauce

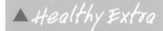 *1 cup mixed baby greens*

1 Remove sausage from casings and form 3 (1 ½-inch) meatballs from each link. Spray large nonstick skillet with nonstick spray and set over medium-high heat. Add meatballs and cook, turning often, until browned on all sides and cooked through, 8–10 minutes.

2 Meanwhile, spread cut sides of rolls evenly with cranberry sauce. Fill rolls evenly with greens and meatballs making 4 sandwiches.

PER SERVING (1 sandwich): 200 grams, 308 Cal, 11 g Total Fat, 0 g Sat Fat, 0 g Trans Fat, 51 mg Chol, 761 mg Sod, 36 g Carb, 13 g Sugar, 4 g Fib, 18 g Prot, 46 mg Calc.

Healthy Extra

Serve the sandwiches with a handful of celery sticks or baby carrots alongside.

Tofu-Tomato Salad with Sesame and Basil

 2 cups cherry or grape tomatoes, halved

1 tablespoon seasoned rice vinegar

2 teaspoons canola oil

2 teaspoons reduced-sodium soy sauce

¼ teaspoon Asian (dark) sesame oil

⅛ teaspoon black pepper

Pinch salt

7 fresh basil leaves

 1 pound reduced-fat soft silken tofu, drained and cut into 8 slices

1 Stir together tomatoes, vinegar, canola oil, soy sauce, sesame oil, pepper, and salt in medium bowl. Cut 3 of the basil leaves into thin slices; add to tomato mixture.

2 Divide tofu evenly among 4 serving plates; top evenly with tomato mixture. Top each serving with 1 of the remaining basil leaves.

PER SERVING (1 plate): 200 grams, 91 Cal, 4 g Total Fat, 0 g Sat Fat, 0 g Trans Fat, 0 mg Chol, 259 mg Sod, 8 g Carb, 3 g Sugar, 1 g Fib, 7 g Prot, 384 mg Calc.

F.Y.I.

Silken tofu is as smooth as custard and almost as soft. It is delicious served for breakfast with fresh fruit and a drizzle of honey, blended into a smoothie, and in cool salads such as this one.

Gingery White Bean and Carrot Soup

SERVES 4

▲ **2 cups reduced-sodium chicken broth**

1 cup carrot juice

▲ **1 (15 ½-ounce) can no-salt-added cannellini (white kidney) beans, rinsed and drained**

5 slices Canadian bacon, halved and thinly sliced

1 tablespoon finely chopped crystallized ginger

¼ teaspoon salt

⅛ teaspoon black pepper

1 tablespoon chopped fresh flat-leaf parsley

1 Combine all ingredients except parsley in large saucepan. Set over medium-high heat, cover, and bring to boil. Reduce heat and simmer, covered, 5 minutes.

2 Divide soup evenly among 4 serving bowls and sprinkle evenly with parsley.

PER SERVING (1 ¼ cups): 230 grams, 189 Cal, 4 g Total Fat, 1 g Sat Fat, 0 g Trans Fat, 17 mg Chol, 709 mg Sod, 23 g Carb, 2 g Sugar, 4 g Fib, 15 g Prot, 57 mg Calc.

F.Y.I.

Fresh carrot juice is available in many supermarkets. Look for it in the produce section or in the refrigerator case near the orange juice.

Coconut-Curry Tomato Soup

SERVES 4

1 teaspoon canola oil

1 ¼ teaspoons Thai red curry paste

 2 (14 ½-ounce) cans petite diced tomatoes

1 cup light (reduced-fat) coconut milk

¾ cup water

¼ teaspoon salt

2 teaspoons lime juice

⅓ cup fresh cilantro leaves

1 Heat oil in large saucepan over medium heat. Add curry paste and cook, stirring constantly, until fragrant, about 1 minute. Stir in tomatoes, coconut milk, water, and salt; bring to boil. Reduce heat and simmer, covered, 3 minutes. Remove from heat and stir in lime juice.

2 Divide soup evenly among 4 serving bowls and sprinkle evenly with cilantro.

5 PointsPlus® value ™ Per Serving

PER SERVING (generous 1 ¼ cups): 275 grams, 172 Cal, 13 g Total Fat, 11 g Sat Fat, 0 g Trans Fat, 0 mg Chol, 670 mg Sod, 12 g Carb, 6 g Sugar, 2 g Fib, 3 g Prot, 46 mg Calc.

▲ Healthy Extra

To give the soup more protein, add 6 ounces firm tofu, cubed, during the last 3 minutes of cooking. The per-serving **PointsPlus** value will increase by **1**.

*Coconut-Curry
Tomato Soup*

Chilled Avocado and Cucumber Soup

SERVES 4

3 1/2 cups plain low-fat yogurt

1 garlic clove, minced

1/2 teaspoon ground coriander

1/2 teaspoon salt

1/4 teaspoon black pepper

▲ **1 English (seedless) cucumber, peeled, seeded, and thinly sliced**

1 Hass avocado, pitted, peeled, and finely chopped

1/3 cup plus 1 tablespoon chopped fresh dill

1 Combine yogurt, garlic, coriander, salt, and pepper in large bowl. Stir in cucumber, avocado, and 1/3 cup of the dill.

2 Divide soup evenly among 4 serving bowls and sprinkle evenly with remaining 1 tablespoon dill.

PER SERVING (generous 1 1/4 cups): 225 grams, 200 Cal, 9 g Total Fat, 3 g Sat Fat, 0 g Trans Fat, 13 mg Chol, 445 mg Sod, 20 g Carb, 16 g Sugar, 3 g Fib, 12 g Prot, 408 mg Calc.

▲ **Healthy Extra**

To add more color and flavor to the soup, top each serving with chopped tomato.

Pepper Steak and Watercress Sandwiches

SERVES 4

- ▲ *2 (¹/₄-pound) filet mignon steaks, trimmed*
- *¹/₂ teaspoon salt*
- *¹/₂ teaspoon coarsely ground black pepper*
- ▲ *¹/₄ cup plain fat-free Greek yogurt*
- *1 teaspoon prepared horseradish*
- *4 (2-ounce) whole grain rolls, split and toasted*
- ▲ *1 cup watercress sprigs*

1 Sprinkle steaks with salt and pepper. Spray large nonstick skillet with nonstick spray and set over medium-high heat. Add steaks and cook until instant-read thermometer inserted into center of each steak registers 145°F for medium, 2–3 minutes on each side. Transfer to cutting board and let stand 3 minutes. Slice steaks into ³/₄-inch-thick slices.

2 Meanwhile, stir together yogurt and horseradish in small bowl.

3 Spread cut sides of rolls evenly with yogurt mixture. Fill rolls evenly with steak and watercress.

6 PointsPlus® value ™
Per Serving

PER SERVING *(1 sandwich): 160 grams, 244 Cal, 6 g Total Fat, 2 g Sat Fat, 0 g Trans Fat, 34 mg Chol, 90 mg Sod, 30 g Carb, 5 g Sugar, 4 g Fib, 19 g Prot, 90 mg Calc.*

▲ *Healthy Extra*

Add tomato and cucumber slices to the sandwiches.

Buy Food Fast

Supermarkets want you to spend a lot of time in the store. The longer you're there, the more money you spend on items you don't really need. Here's how to get in and out of the store quickly:

■ **Go When It's Slow.** Do your shopping at your convenience, but when it's slow at the store. Weekends and right after work are, of course, the busiest times. Why not choose early morning or an evening during the week when you don't have other commitments and can do your shopping after dinner? The after-work rush will have subsided and you can breeze through the aisles. If you have a flexible work schedule, visit the store mid-morning or mid-afternoon.

■ **Be Strategic.** Find a time that is best for you to shop alone. If you bring your kids, you may get distracted, walk slower, or buy items that you—and they— don't need.

■ **Stay Focused.** With flyers, signs, and shelf hangtags, not to mention those enticing free samples, the supermarket can be so distracting that you blow your whole afternoon shopping. When you shop, concentrate and keep your focus on your list, finding the items on it, and passing through the checkout without succumbing to tempting sale items that you don't need.

■ **Think Small.** Huge warehouse-size stores offer tremendous variety, but if 30 aisles of groceries seem overwhelming, downsize to a smaller market in your neighborhood. You'll get your shopping done quicker and probably save money, too, since there will be fewer flashing coupon dispensers, sausage samples, and end-of-aisle promotions.

■ **Do It All Now.** If you are ready to check out and realize you've forgotten an item that's on the other side of the store, retrace your steps and get it now. It will save more time than if you have to make a special trip later in the week. And, think of the exercise you're getting.

Pasta with Watercress and Ginger

SERVES 4

▲ **1 ½ cups whole wheat macaroni**

2 teaspoons canola oil

2 tablespoons minced crystallized ginger

½ teaspoon salt

¼ teaspoon red pepper flakes

▲ **1 bunch watercress, tough stems discarded and tender sprigs chopped**

1 Cook pasta according to package directions, omitting salt if desired; drain and keep warm.

2 Meanwhile, heat oil in large nonstick skillet over medium heat. Add ginger, salt, and pepper flakes and cook, stirring constantly, until fragrant, about 1 minute. Remove skillet from heat. Add pasta and watercress and stir just until watercress is wilted, about 1 minute.

PER SERVING (1 cup): 140 grams, 182 Cal, 3 g Total Fat, 0 g Sat Fat, 0 g Trans Fat, 0 mg Chol, 308 mg Sod, 35 g Carb, 4 g Sugar, 3 g Fib, 6 g Prot, 60 mg Calc.

F.Y.I.

Crystallized ginger is a pantry staple for which you'll find many uses. Finely mince the ginger and add it to stir-fries, salads, stews, or pasta dishes for an explosion of ginger flavor and just a touch of sweetness.

Couscous with Chickpeas and Oranges

SERVES 4

▲ **1 ¼ cups reduced-sodium chicken broth**

▲ **1 cup canned chickpeas, rinsed and drained**

¼ teaspoon salt

⅛ teaspoon black pepper

▲ **1 cup whole wheat couscous**

▲ **2 large navel oranges**

¼ cup thinly sliced fresh mint

1 tablespoon olive oil

1 tablespoon seasoned rice vinegar

1 Combine broth, chickpeas, salt, and pepper in medium saucepan; bring to boil. Add couscous, cover, and remove from heat. Let stand 5 minutes.

2 Meanwhile, with sharp knife, peel oranges, removing all white pith. Cut oranges into rounds; cut rounds into quarters. Place oranges in large bowl. Add couscous mixture, mint, oil, and vinegar; toss to combine.

PER SERVING (1 ¼ cups): 200 grams, 236 Cal, 5 g Total Fat, 1 g Sat Fat, 0 g Trans Fat, 0 mg Chol, 383 mg Sod, 42 g Carb, 8 g Sugar, 7 g Fib, 9 g Prot, 57 mg Calc.

Smoky Kasha with Scallions

1 tablespoon olive oil

¾ teaspoon smoked or regular paprika

▲ **1 cup kasha**

¼ teaspoon salt

⅛ teaspoon black pepper

▲ **2 cups reduced-sodium chicken broth**

▲ **2 scallions, thinly sliced**

1 Heat oil in large saucepan over medium heat. Add paprika and cook, stirring constantly, until fragrant, about 1 minute. Stir in kasha, salt, and pepper and cook, stirring constantly, until kasha is coated, about 1 minute.

2 Add broth to saucepan. Increase heat to high and bring to boil. Reduce heat, cover, and simmer until most of liquid is absorbed, 8–10 minutes. Transfer to serving bowl; stir in scallions.

PER SERVING (generous ¾ cup): 150 grams, 195 Cal, 5 g Total Fat, 1 g Sat Fat, 0 g Trans Fat, 0 mg Chol, 187 mg Sod, 33 g Carb, 0 g Sugar, 5 g Fib, 7 g Prot, 18 mg Calc. .

F.Y.I.

Smoked paprika from Spain is an **easy way to add a complex flavor** to your cooking. The peppers are smoked before being ground to give it its distinctive fragrance.

*Spicy Bulgur and
Carrots with Harissa*

Spicy Bulgur and Carrots with Harissa

2 cups water

▲ **1 cup quick-cooking bulgur**

¼ teaspoon salt

⅛ teaspoon black pepper

▲ **1 cup coarsely shredded carrots**

¾ teaspoon harissa

½ cup chopped fresh cilantro

1 Combine water, bulgur, salt, and pepper in large saucepan; bring to boil over high heat. Reduce heat and simmer, covered, until bulgur is tender, 8–10 minutes.

2 Add carrots and harissa to saucepan and cook, stirring constantly, until carrots are heated through, about 1 minute. Transfer to serving bowl; stir in cilantro.

PER SERVING (1 cup): 85 grams, 132 Cal, 1 g Total Fat, 0 g Sat Fat, 0 g Trans Fat, 0 mg Chol, 175 mg Sod, 29 g Carb, 1 g Sugar, 7 g Fib, 5 g Prot, 25 mg Calc.

▲ *Healthy Extra*

Add 1 cup thawed frozen green peas when you add the carrots (the per-serving **PointsPlus** value will increase by **1**).

Polenta with Mozzarella and Tapenade

SERVES 4

▲ **1 (16-ounce) tube refrigerated fat-free plain polenta, cut into 12 slices**

¼ cup shredded part-skim mozzarella cheese

Black pepper

1 tablespoon purchased tapenade

2 tablespoons chopped fresh flat-leaf parsley

1 Preheat broiler. Spray large baking sheet with nonstick spray. Arrange polenta in single layer on baking sheet. Top each slice with 1 teaspoon of the mozzarella and small pinch of pepper.

2 Broil polenta 4 inches from heat until cheese is melted and polenta is heated through, about 5 minutes.

3 Transfer polenta to serving platter. Top each slice with ¼ teaspoon of the tapenade and sprinkle evenly with parsley.

PER SERVING (3 slices): 160 grams, 111 Cal, 2 g Total Fat, 1 g Sat Fat, 0 g Trans Fat, 4 mg Chol, 460 mg Sod, 18 g Carb, 1 g Sugar, 1 g Fib, 4 g Prot, 56 mg Calc.

F.Y.I.

A sprinkle of chopped fresh herbs gives this dish a boost of flavor. Instead of the parsley, sprinkle on whatever herbs you have on hand. Try basil, oregano, thyme, or marjoram.

Cherry Tomato and Baby Spinach Sauté

SERVES 4

▲ **4 cups cherry or grape tomatoes, halved**

1 tablespoon olive oil

1 teaspoon balsamic vinegar

1/4 teaspoon salt

1/8 teaspoon black pepper

▲ **2 cups baby spinach**

1 Combine tomatoes, oil, vinegar, salt, and pepper in large nonstick skillet; cook over medium-high heat, stirring often, until tomatoes are softened, about 5 minutes.

2 Add spinach to skillet and cook, stirring constantly, just until wilted, about 1 minute.

PER SERVING (³⁄4 cup): 130 grams, 61 Cal, 4 g Total Fat, 1 g Sat Fat, 0 g Trans Fat, 0 mg Chol, 163 mg Sod, 7 g Carb, 4 g Sugar, 2 g Fib, 1 g Prot, 20 mg Calc.

▲ *Healthy Extra*

Turn this into a main dish by serving it over broiled sirloin steak. A 3-ounce serving of broiled sirloin will increase the **PointsPlus** value by **3**.

Sautéed Zucchini and Tomatoes with Cardamom

SERVES 4

1 tablespoon olive oil

▲ **3 medium zucchini, halved lengthwise and thinly sliced**

¼ cup water

¼ teaspoon salt

¼ teaspoon ground cardamom

⅛ teaspoon black pepper

▲ **1 (14-ounce) can petite diced tomatoes, drained**

1 Heat oil in large nonstick skillet over medium-high heat. Add zucchini, water, salt, cardamom, and pepper. Cook, stirring often, until zucchini is softened and most of liquid is evaporated, about 7 minutes.

2 Add tomatoes to skillet and cook, stirring constantly, until heated through, about 2 minutes.

PER SERVING *(1 cup): 125 grams, 77 Cal, 4 g Total Fat, 1 g Sat Fat, 0 g Trans Fat, 0 mg Chol, 382 mg Sod, 10 g Carb, 6 g Sugar, 2 g Fib, 3 g Prot, 39 mg Calc.*

Broccoli with Spicy Honey-Sesame Sauce

SERVES 4

▲ **4 cups small broccoli florets**

2 tablespoons reduced-sodium soy sauce

1 tablespoon honey

1 tablespoon toasted sesame seeds

½ teaspoon Asian (dark) sesame oil

Pinch red pepper flakes

1 Fill large saucepan two-thirds full with water and bring to boil; add broccoli. Cook until broccoli is crisp-tender, about 3 minutes; drain.

2 Meanwhile, stir together soy sauce, honey, sesame seeds, oil, and pepper flakes in medium bowl. Add broccoli and toss to coat.

PER SERVING *(1 cup): 75 grams, 58 Cal, 2 g Total Fat, 0 g Sat Fat, 0 g Trans Fat, 0 mg Chol, 290 mg Sod, 9 g Carb, 4 g Sugar, 2 g Fib, 3 g Prot, 43 mg Calc.*

Coconut-Cumin Green Beans

SERVES 4

▲ **1 pound green beans, trimmed**

2 teaspoons canola oil

1/3 cup flaked unsweetened coconut

1/2 teaspoon cumin seeds

1/4 teaspoon salt

1/8 teaspoon black pepper

1 Bring medium saucepan of water to boil over high heat. Add beans and cook just until crisp-tender, about 3 minutes. Drain.

2 Meanwhile, heat oil in large skillet over medium heat. Add coconut and cumin and cook, stirring constantly, until coconut is toasted, 1–2 minutes. Add beans, salt, and pepper and cook, stirring constantly, until heated through, about 1 minute.

PER SERVING *(generous 3/4 cup): 75 grams, 110 Cal, 7 g Total Fat, 4 g Sat Fat, 0 g Trans Fat, 0 mg Chol, 155 mg Sod, 10 g Carb, 2 g Sugar, 5 g Fib, 3 g Prot, 44 mg Calc.*

F.Y.I.

Flaked unsweetened coconut is available in the ethnic section of large supermarkets. It's great to add to granola or trail mix or to substitute for flaked sweetened coconut in any recipe where you want a little less sweetness.

Lemony Fennel and Radicchio

2 teaspoons olive oil

▲ *2 medium fennel bulbs, trimmed and thinly sliced*

¼ teaspoon salt

⅛ teaspoon black pepper

¼ cup water

▲ *1 cup finely shredded radicchio*

2 tablespoons chopped fresh flat-leaf parsley

2 teaspoons grated lemon zest

2 teaspoons lemon juice

1 Heat oil in large nonstick skillet over medium heat. Add fennel, salt, and pepper and cook, stirring constantly, about 1 minute. Add water, cover, and cook, stirring occasionally, until fennel begins to soften, about 3 minutes.

2 Uncover skillet, increase heat to medium-high, and cook, stirring constantly, until most of liquid is evaporated and fennel is tender, about 2 minutes. Remove from heat and stir in radicchio, parsley, and lemon zest and juice.

PER SERVING (1 cup): 75 grams, 61 Cal, 3 g Total Fat, 0 g Sat Fat, 0 g Trans Fat, 0 mg Chol, 210 mg Sod, 10 g Carb, 0 g Sugar, 4 g Fib, 2 g Prot, 64 mg Calc.

▲ Healthy Extra

Add 1 large sweet onion, thinly sliced, with the fennel in step 1.

Lemony Fennel and
Radicchio

Goat Cheese and Olive Pitas

SERVES 4

1/4 cup soft goat cheese

6 (2 1/2-inch) whole wheat mini pita breads, halved and toasted

2 tablespoons purchased tapenade

▲ 1/4 cup cherry tomatoes, chopped

2 tablespoons chopped fresh basil or flat-leaf parsley

Spread 1 teaspoon of the goat cheese on each pita half, then spread each with 1/2 teaspoon of the tapenade. Sprinkle pitas evenly with tomatoes and basil.

PER SERVING (3 pita halves): 15 grams, 146 Cal, 5 g Total Fat, 2 g Sat Fat, 0 g Trans Fat, 7 mg Chol, 390 mg Sod, 19 g Carb, 0 g Sugar, 3 g Fib, 7 g Prot, 23 mg Calc.

Asian Hummus

SERVES 4

▲ 1 (15 1/2-ounce) can chickpeas, rinsed and drained

2 tablespoons water

2 teaspoons reduced-sodium soy sauce

1 garlic clove, chopped

3/4 teaspoon grated peeled fresh ginger

1/2 teaspoon Asian (dark) sesame oil

1/8–1/4 teaspoon hot pepper sauce

1/4 cup loosely packed fresh cilantro leaves

Place chickpeas, water, soy sauce, garlic, ginger, oil, and hot sauce in food processor and pulse until smooth. Add cilantro and pulse until chopped. (Hummus may be prepared and refrigerated, covered, up to 3 days.)

PER SERVING (generous 1/4 cup): 68 grams, , 95 Cal, 2 g Total Fat, 0 g Sat Fat, 0 g Trans Fat, 0 mg Chol, 341 mg Sod, 15 g Carb, 2 g Sugar, 4 g Fib, 5 g Prot, 20 mg Calc. .

Apples with Cheese, Quince Paste, and Walnuts

SERVES 4

¼ *cup light cream cheese (Neufchâtel)*

▲ *1 large Granny Smith or Gala apple, cored and cut into 12 wedges*

1 ¾ ounces quince paste, thinly sliced and cut into 12 strips

¼ *cup chopped toasted walnuts*

Spread 1 teaspoon of the cream cheese on each apple wedge. Top each wedge with strip of quince paste. Arrange apple slices on serving plate and sprinkle with evenly walnuts.

PER SERVING *(3 wedges): 75 grams, 141 Cal, 7 g Total Fat, 2 g Sat Fat, 0 g Trans Fat, 8 mg Chol, 75 mg Sod, 18 g Carb, 13 g Sugar, 3 g Fib, 3 g Prot, 34 mg Calc.*

F.Y.I.

Quince paste is a dense sweet puree of quince fruit that is traditionally served with Manchego cheese in Spain. It pairs well with any creamy cheese or nuts.

Strawberry-Mascarpone Toasts

Strawberry-Mascarpone Toasts

SERVES 6

▲ **1 cup medium strawberries, hulled and thinly sliced**

½ teaspoon sugar

½ teaspoon lemon juice

4 tablespoons mascarpone cheese

1 (10-ounce) multigrain baguette, cut on diagonal into 12 slices and toasted

1 tablespoon chopped fresh mint (optional)

1 Toss together strawberries, sugar, and lemon juice in small bowl.

2 Spread 1 teaspoon of the mascarpone onto each baguette slice; top evenly with strawberry mixture. Sprinkle toasts evenly with mint, if using.

PER SERVING *(2 toasts): 91 grams, 214 Cal, 10 g Total Fat, 5 g Sat Fat, 0 g Trans Fat, 23 mg Chol, 269 mg Sod, 26 g Carb, 3 g Sugar, 3 g Fib, 7 g Prot, 31 mg Calc.*

F.Y.I.

Mascarpone is a soft, spreadable Italian cheese. If you have trouble finding it, you can substitute soft reduced-fat cream cheese in this recipe.

Spicy Guacamole Snack Cakes

1 Hass avocado, halved, pitted, and peeled

▲ **2 tablespoons minced red onion**

1 tablespoon chopped fresh cilantro

2 teaspoons minced pickled jalapeño peppers

2 teaspoons lime juice

¼ teaspoon salt

4 (4-inch) brown rice cakes

▲ **½ cup chopped tomato**

Coarsely mash avocado in medium bowl. Add onion, cilantro, jalapeño, lime juice, and salt and stir until combined. Spread avocado mixture evenly on rice cakes and top evenly with tomato.

PER SERVING (1 topped rice cake): 58 grams, 138 Cal, 6 g Total Fat, 1 g Sat Fat, 0 g Trans Fat, 0 mg Chol, 222 mg Sod, 21 g Carb, 1 g Sugar, 3 g Fib, 2 g Prot, 13 mg Calc.

▲ **Healthy Extra**

To make this a more substantial treat, enjoy the snack cakes with a sliced Kirby cucumber.

Lemon-Herb Snack Mix

SERVES 6

2 teaspoons unsalted butter

1 teaspoon olive oil

1 1/2 teaspoons grated lemon zest

3/4 teaspoon garlic powder

1/2 teaspoon dried thyme

1/4 teaspoon coarsely ground black pepper

1/8 teaspoon salt

2 cups 7–whole grain puffed cereal

1 1/2 cups wheat cereal squares

1 1/2 cups whole wheat pretzel sticks

1 Combine butter and oil in large microwavable bowl; microwave on High until melted, 15–20 seconds. Stir in lemon zest, garlic powder, thyme, pepper, and salt. Add cereals and pretzels and stir until well coated.

2 Microwave snack mix on High, uncovered, 3 minutes, stirring after each minute. Spread snack mix onto paper towels to cool. Store in airtight container up to 2 weeks.

8 PointsPlus® value
Per Serving

PER SERVING (1/2 cup): 22 grams, 306 Cal, 4 g Total Fat, 1 g Sat Fat, 0 g Trans Fat, 3 mg Chol, 296 mg Sod, 64 g Carb, 2 g Sugar, 7 g Fib, 9 g Prot, 52 mg Calc.

F.Y.I.

Different models of microwaves vary widely in wattage and cooking times, so **check the snack mix often as it cooks** to prevent burning the cereal.

Chocolate Sorbet with Warm Cherries

2 teaspoons canola oil

1 tablespoon sugar

Pinch salt

▲ **2 cups fresh sweet cherries, pitted or thawed frozen unsweetened cherries**

Pinch grated lime zest

1 ½ teaspoons lime juice

1 pint chocolate sorbet

1 Heat oil in large nonstick skillet over medium heat. Add sugar and salt and cook, stirring constantly, until sugar is almost dissolved, about 2 minutes. Add cherries and cook, stirring constantly, until softened, 2–3 minutes. Remove from heat and stir in lime zest and juice.

2 Place ½-cup scoop of the sorbet in each of 4 serving bowls; spoon cherries evenly over sorbet.

PER SERVING (½ cup sorbet + scant ⅓ cup cherries): 200 grams, 167 Cal, 2 g Total Fat, 0 g Sat Fat, 0 g Trans Fat, 0 mg Chol, 144 mg Sod, 34 g Carb, 28 g Sugar, 3 g Fib, 2 g Prot, 10 mg Calc.

F.Y.I.

Instead of the chocolate sorbet, you can serve the cherries over a fruit-flavored sorbet or low-fat vanilla ice cream or frozen yogurt.

*Chocolate Sorbet with
Warm Cherries*

Strawberries with Ginger-Lemon Sugar

SERVES 4

2 tablespoons sugar

1 teaspoon finely chopped crystallized ginger

¹⁄₂ teaspoon grated lemon zest

▲ **1 (1-pound) container strawberries, hulled and quartered**

1 Process sugar, ginger, and lemon zest in coffee or spice grinder until finely ground.

2 Place strawberries in medium bowl; sprinkle with sugar mixture and toss to coat. Let stand until berries begin to release their juices, about 5 minutes. Serve at room temperature.

PER SERVING (¾ cup): 125 grams, 56 Cal, 0 g Total Fat, 0 g Sat Fat, 0 g Trans Fat, 0 mg Chol, 2 mg Sod, 14 g Carb, 11 g Sugar, 2 g Fib, 1 g Prot, 20 mg Calc.

Warm Caramel Pineapple with Raspberries

SERVES 4

¹⁄₂ cup fat-free sugar-free caramel ice-cream topping

▲ **3 cups (¹⁄₂-inch) cubes fresh pineapple**

Pinch salt

▲ **1 cup fresh raspberries**

1 tablespoon lime juice

1 Bring caramel topping to simmer in large nonstick skillet over medium heat. Add pineapple and salt, increase heat to medium-high, and bring to boil. Boil, stirring often, until pineapple is softened, about 8 minutes.

2 Remove skillet from heat and stir in raspberries and lime juice. Divide evenly among 4 serving bowls and serve at once.

PER SERVING (1 cup): 150 grams, 220 Cal, 0 g Total Fat, 0 g Sat Fat, 0 g Trans Fat, 0 mg Chol, 104 mg Sod, 58 g Carb, 24 g Sugar, 5 g Fib, 2 g Prot, 38 mg Calc.

Mixed Berries with Honey-Caramel Sauce

⅔ **cup honey**

▲ **2 tablespoons fat-free half-and-half**

Pinch salt

1/2 teaspoon lemon juice

▲ **4 cups mixed fresh berries (such as blueberries, raspberries, and blackberries)**

1 Bring honey to boil in medium saucepan over medium-high heat. Reduce heat to medium and boil, whisking often, until darkened and fragrant, 3–4 minutes (being careful not to burn honey). Remove saucepan from heat. Slowly and carefully whisk in half-and-half and salt (mixture may look curdled).

2 Return saucepan to medium heat; return to boil. Boil, whisking often, until slightly thickened, about 5 minutes (sauce will thicken further as it cools slightly).

3 Pour sauce through small fine strainer set over small heatproof bowl; whisk in lemon juice.

4 Divide berries evenly among 8 serving bowls; drizzle evenly with sauce.

PER SERVING (½ *cup berries + 1 tablespoon sauce): 83 grams, 125 Cal, 0 g Total Fat, 0 g Sat Fat, 0 g Trans Fat, 0 mg Chol, 23 mg Sod, 33 g Carb, 29 g Sugar, 3 g Fib, 1 g Prot, 17 mg Calc. .*

Ice Cream with Chocolate Sauce and Peanut Brittle

Ice Cream with Chocolate Sauce and Peanut Brittle

▲ **¼ cup fat-free half-and-half**

2 teaspoons packed brown sugar

Pinch salt

2 ounces semisweet chocolate, finely chopped

¼ teaspoon vanilla extract

1 pint fat-free chocolate ice cream

2 tablespoons chopped peanut brittle

1 Combine half-and-half, brown sugar, and salt in small saucepan. Bring just to boil over medium-high heat, stirring to dissolve brown sugar. Remove from heat, add chocolate, and whisk until smooth.

2 Return saucepan to medium-high heat and return to boil, whisking constantly. Boil, whisking constantly, until slightly thickened, about 1 minute. Remove from heat and whisk in vanilla.

3 Place ½-cup scoop of the ice cream in each of 4 serving bowls; drizzle evenly with sauce and sprinkle with peanut brittle. Serve at once.

PER SERVING *(½ cup ice cream, 2 tablespoons sauce, + ½ tablespoon peanut brittle): 140 grams, 213 Cal, 7 g Total Fat, 4 g Sat Fat, 0 g Trans Fat, 6 mg Chol, 168 mg Sod, 39 g Carb, 29 g Sugar, 4 g Fib, 5 g Prot, 102 mg Calc.*

▲ *Healthy Extra*

To make this dessert more filling and colorful, add ½ cup fresh raspberries, blueberries, or sliced strawberries to each serving.

Cannoli Cream and Cookies

SERVES 4

▲ **2 cups fat-free ricotta cheese**

2 tablespoons sugar

¼ teaspoon vanilla extract

¼ teaspoon grated orange zest

⅓ cup golden raisins

3 tablespoons chopped pistachios

2 tablespoons semisweet mini-chocolate chips

4 purchased low-fat biscotti cookies

1 Place ricotta, sugar, vanilla, and orange zest in food processor and process until smooth, 1–2 minutes. Transfer ricotta mixture to medium bowl; stir in raisins, 2 tablespoons of the pistachios, and the chocolate chips.

2 Spoon ricotta mixture into serving bowls and sprinkle evenly with remaining 1 tablespoon pistachios. Serve biscotti alongside.

 PER SERVING (generous ½ cup ricotta mixture + 1 cookie): 170 grams, 288 Cal, 6 g Total Fat, 1 g Sat Fat, 0 g Trans Fat, 20 mg Chol, 159 mg Sod, 43 g Carb, 27 g Sugar, 3 g Fib, 13 g Prot, 215 mg Calc.

Affogato

SERVES 4

1 pint fat-free vanilla ice cream

½ cup hot espresso or very strong brewed coffee

Place ½-cup scoop of the ice cream in each of 4 serving bowls. Pour hot espresso evenly over ice cream and serve at once.

 PER SERVING (½ cup ice cream + 2 tablespoons espresso): 75 grams, 93 Cal, 2 g Total Fat, 1 g Sat Fat, 0 g Trans Fat, 5 mg Chol, 50 mg Sod, 21 g Carb, 14 g Sugar, 4 g Fib, 2 g Prot, 84 mg Calc.

Figs Poached with Lemon, Honey, and Thyme

SERVES 4

1 ¹/₂ cups apple cider or unsweetened apple juice

4 (2-inch-long) strips lemon zest, removed with vegetable peeler

1 tablespoon honey

¹/₂ teaspoon fresh thyme leaves

Pinch salt

¹/₂ pound dried figs, stemmed and cut into wedges

¹/₄ teaspoon vanilla extract

1 Combine cider, lemon zest, honey, thyme, and salt in large saucepan. Set over medium-high heat, cover, and bring to boil; boil 3 minutes.

2 Add figs to saucepan, reduce heat, and simmer, partially covered, until figs are softened, about 3 minutes. Remove from heat and stir in vanilla. Serve warm or at room temperature.

PER SERVING *(generous ¹/₃ cup): 60 grams, 203 Cal, 1 g Total Fat, 0 g Sat Fat, 0 g Trans Fat, 0 mg Chol, 52 mg Sod, 52 g Carb, 41 g Sugar, 6 g Fib, 2 g Prot, 93 mg Calc.*

▲ Healthy Extra

Serve the figs with ¹/₃ cup plain fat-free yogurt for an additional **1 PointsPlus** value per serving.

Peaches and Raspberries with Lemon Crunch

SERVES 4

▲ **4 medium peaches, halved, pitted, and sliced**

▲ **1 cup fresh raspberries**

1 tablespoon granulated sugar

3 rough-cut brown sugar cubes

½ teaspoon grated lemon zest

1 Toss together peaches, raspberries, and sugar in medium bowl.

2 In spice grinder or with mortar and pestle, finely grind sugar cubes and lemon zest.

3 Divide peach mixture evenly among 4 serving bowls; sprinkle evenly with sugar cube mixture and serve at once.

PER SERVING *(1 cup fruit + ¾ teaspoon sugar mixture): 200 grams, 77 Cal, 0 g Total Fat, 0 g Sat Fat, 0 g Trans Fat, 0 mg Chol, 1 mg Sod, 19 g Carb, 7 g Sugar, 4 g Fib, 1 g Prot, 11 mg Calc.*

F.Y.I.

You can use 4 medium nectarines or 8 small apricots in this recipe instead of the peaches. If brown sugar cubes are unavailable, **use 1 tablespoon turbinado (raw) sugar instead.**

Peaches and Raspberries
with Lemon Crunch

Warm Coconut Rice with Mango

SERVES 4

½ cup light (reduced-fat) coconut milk

1 tablespoon packed light brown sugar

Pinch salt

▲ *1 (8.8-ounce) package cooked brown rice (about 1 ¾ cups)*

▲ *1 large mango, peeled, pitted, and sliced*

4 teaspoons chopped pistachios

1 Combine coconut milk, brown sugar, and salt in medium saucepan. Bring to boil over medium-high heat. Add rice and return to boil. Cook, stirring constantly, until most of liquid is absorbed, about 3 minutes.

2 Divide rice evenly among 4 serving bowls; arrange mango slices evenly around rice. Sprinkle with pistachios. Serve at once.

6 PointsPlus© value

Per Serving

PER SERVING (⅓ cup rice, about 4 mango slices, + 1 teaspoon pistachios): 240 grams, 212 Cal, 8 g Total Fat, 6 g Sat Fat, 0 g Trans Fat, 0 mg Chol, 43 mg Sod, 34 g Carb, 11 g Sugar, 3 g Fib, 3 g Prot, 24 mg Calc.

▲ Healthy Extra

Make the rice even more of a tropical treat by serving it with 1 small papaya, peeled, seeded, and sliced along with the mango.

Coriander Toasts with Strawberries and Yogurt

▲ **1 (1-pound) container strawberries, hulled and sliced**

7 tablespoons sugar

¼ teaspoon grated lemon zest

Pinch salt

▲ **1 cup plain fat-free Greek yogurt**

¼ teaspoon vanilla extract

1 teaspoon ground coriander

6 slices whole grain bread, toasted and crusts trimmed and discarded

1 Stir together strawberries, 2 tablespoons of the sugar, the lemon zest, and salt in medium bowl.

2 Stir together yogurt, 1 tablespoon of the remaining sugar, and the vanilla in small bowl. Stir together remaining 4 tablespoons sugar and the coriander on large plate.

3 Lightly coat both sides of each toast slice with vegetable oil cooking spray. Cut each slice diagonally in half. Dip both sides of each toast triangle in coriander mixture to coat; shake off excess. Divide toast evenly among 4 serving plates; top evenly with berry mixture and dollop evenly with yogurt mixture.

PER SERVING *(3 toast triangles, ¾ cup strawberries, + ¼ cup yogurt mixture): 170 grams, 231 Cal, 3 g Total Fat, 0 g Sat Fat, 0 g Trans Fat, 0 mg Chol, 257 mg Sod, 44 g Carb, 26 g Sugar, 5 g Fib, 11 g Prot, 101 mg Calc.*

Chocolate-Hazelnut Raspberry Toasts

Chocolate-Hazelnut Raspberry Toasts

$1/4$ **cup chopped hazelnuts**

2 ounces semisweet chocolate, chopped

▲ $1/4$ **cup fat-free half-and-half**

1 $1/2$ tablespoons packed brown sugar

Pinch salt

8 slices whole grain bread, toasted

▲ **2 (6-ounce) packages fresh raspberries**

Superfine sugar for dusting (optional)

1 Place hazelnuts in mini food processor and process until paste forms, about 3 minutes. Add chocolate and pulse until chocolate is finely ground. Leave mixture in food processor.

2 Meanwhile, combine half-and-half, brown sugar, and salt in small saucepan and bring just to boil over medium heat, stirring to dissolve brown sugar.

3 With motor running, add half-and-half mixture through feed tube and process, scraping down bowl once or twice, until mixture is very smooth, 3–4 minutes. Transfer to small bowl and let cool slightly. For thicker consistency, refrigerate hazelnut spread, covered, 30 minutes.

4 Spread toast evenly with hazelnut mixture; cut each slice diagonally in half and top with raspberries. Dust with sugarfine sugar, if using.

PER SERVING (2 toast triangles): 91 grams, 164 Cal, 6 g Total Fat, 2 g Sat Fat, 0 g Trans Fat, 0 mg Chol, 165 mg Sod, 26 g Carb, 11 g Sugar, 5 g Fib, 5 g Prot, 84 mg Calc.

Honey-Glazed Nectarines with Ricotta and Amaretti

SERVES 4

▲ **4 medium nectarines, halved and pitted**

3 tablespoons honey

2 teaspoons lemon juice

Pinch salt

1 cup part-skim ricotta cheese

½ teaspoon grated lemon zest

¼ teaspoon vanilla extract

8 amaretti cookies

F.Y.I.

Amaretti are small almond-flavored Italian cookies. You'll find them in most large supermarkets and specialty stores. If you can't find them, you can **make this dessert with biscotti or gingersnaps instead.**

1 Preheat broiler. Line broiler pan with foil; spray with nonstick spray.

2 Place nectarines, cut-sides up, in prepared broiler pan; broil 5 inches from heat just until heated through, about 2 minutes.

3 Meanwhile, stir together 2 tablespoons of the honey, the lemon juice, and salt in small bowl. Brush nectarines with half of the honey mixture and broil 3 minutes. Brush with remaining honey mixture and broil until nectarines are lightly browned, 2–3 minutes longer.

4 At same time, stir together ricotta, remaining 1 tablespoon honey, the lemon zest, and vanilla in small bowl.

5 Place 2 nectarine halves in each of 4 shallow serving bowls. Top each with ¼ cup of the ricotta mixture. Crumble 4 of the cookies and sprinkle evenly over desserts. Serve each dessert with 1 of the remaining cookies.

PER SERVING (1 dessert): 220 grams, 235 Cal, 6 g Total Fat, 3 g Sat Fat, 0 g Trans Fat, 19 mg Chol, 119 mg Sod, 37 g Carb, 30 g Sugar, 2 g Fib, 9 g Prot, 179 mg Calc.

Nectarines with Chocolate-Balsamic Drizzle

3 tablespoons packed light brown sugar

1 ½ tablespoons balsamic vinegar

Pinch salt

½ ounce bittersweet or semisweet chocolate, finely chopped

▲ **4 medium nectarines, halved, pitted, and sliced**

1 Combine brown sugar, vinegar, and salt in small saucepan and bring to boil over medium-high heat, stirring often. Cook until slightly thickened, 1–2 minutes. Remove from heat, add chocolate, and whisk until smooth. Transfer to small bowl; let stand to cool slightly, whisking occasionally, 5 minutes.

2 Divide nectarines evenly among 4 serving bowls; drizzle evenly with sauce.

PER SERVING *(1 nectarine + scant 1 tablespoon sauce): 120 grams, 125 Cal, 1 g Total Fat, 1 g Sat Fat, 0 g Trans Fat, 0 mg Chol, 41 mg Sod, 28 g Carb, 24 g Sugar, 3 g Fib, 2 g Prot, 19 mg Calc.*

Mango-Berry Meringues with Lime Yogurt

SERVES 4

▲ **1 cup plain fat-free Greek yogurt**

  2 tablespoons sugar

  1 teaspoon grated lime zest

  Pinch salt

▲ **1 large mango, peeled, pitted, and chopped**

▲ **1 (6-ounce) package fresh raspberries**

▲ **1 cup fresh blueberries**

  2 teaspoons lime juice

  4 (2-inch) purchased meringues

1 Stir together yogurt, 1 tablespoon of the sugar, ½ teaspoon of the lime zest, and salt in small bowl.

2 Stir together mango, raspberries, blueberries, remaining 1 tablespoon sugar, and the lime juice in medium bowl.

3 Divide mango mixture evenly among 4 serving bowls; top evenly with yogurt mixture and meringues. Sprinkle yogurt evenly with remaining ½ teaspoon lime zest and serve at once.

PER SERVING *(1 dessert): 220 grams, 159 Cal, 1 g Total Fat, 0 g Sat Fat, 0 g Trans Fat, 0 mg Chol, 91 mg Sod, 33 g Carb, 25 g Sugar, 5 g Fib, 6 g Prot, 56 mg Calc.*

F.Y.I.

If you wish, you can **coarsely crumble the meringues** and sprinkle them over the fruit. That way, you get a bit of crunch and sweetness in every bite.

**Mango-Berry Meringues
with Lime Yogurt**

Mussels in Carrot-Ginger Broth, page 94

Index

Recipes by *PointsPlus* value

 • Strawberries with Ginger-Lemon Sugar, 190

- Asian Hummus, 182
- Berry-Cereal Parfaits with Maple Yogurt, 158
- Broccoli with Spicy Honey-Sesame Sauce, 178
- Cherry Tomato and Baby Spinach Sauté, 177
- Hot-and-Sour Tofu and Vegetable Soup, 144
- Lemony Fennel and Radicchio, 180
- Peaches and Raspberries with Lemon Crunch, 196
- Sautéed Zucchini and Tomatoes with Cardamom, 178
- Tofu-Tomato Salad with Sesame and Basil, 164

- Affogato, 194
- Breakfast Egg Cup with Feta and Chives, 154
- Coconut-Cumin Green Beans, 179
- Mixed Berries with Honey-Caramel Sauce, 191
- Mussels in Carrot-Ginger Broth, 94
- Nectarines with Chocolate-Balsamic Drizzle, 203
- Polenta with Mozzarella and Tapenade, 176
- Rosemary Lamb Chops with Balsamic Tomatoes, 121
- Sesame Grilled Portobellos with Sriracha Mayonnaise, 54
- Spicy Bulgur and Carrots with Harissa, 175
- Thai-Style Chicken and Mushroom Soup, 161

- Apples with Cheese, Quince Paste, and Walnuts, 183
- Chicken and Noodles with Black and Red Pepper, 130
- Chili-Glazed Chicken with Cucumber-Mint Salad, 126

5 PointsPlus value
Per Serving

continued

- Pasta with Watercress and Ginger, 171
- Poppy Seed Chicken and Clementine Salad, 131
- Pork Chops with Carrot-Mint Slaw, 25
- Potato-Crusted Cod with Horseradish Sauce, 44
- Prosciutto-Wrapped Scallop Salad, 48
- Provençal Chicken and Vegetables, 77
- Sirloin with Cherry Tomatoes and Basil, 62
- Smoky Kasha with Scallions, 173
- Steak and Beet Salad with Horseradish Dressing, 110
- Steak Salad with Spinach and Oranges, 112
- Steamed Striped Bass with Sake-Ginger Broth, 47
- Turkey Cutlets with Marsala Mushroom Sauce, 84
- Yogurt-Topped Microwave-Baked Apples, 158

- Chicken and Broccoli with Black Bean Sauce, 129
- Chicken and Polenta with Zucchini-Tomato Sauce, 123
- Coriander Toasts with Strawberries and Yogurt, 199
- Couscous with Chickpeas and Oranges, 172
- Duck Breasts with Balsamic Cranberries, 40
- Figs Poached with Lemon, Honey, and Thyme, 195
- Gaucho Steak with Roasted Poblanos, 16
- Glazed Pork Chops with Poppy Seed Slaw, 69
- Grilled Beef Fattoush Salad, 63
- Grilled Chicken with Tomato Chimichurri Sauce, 29
- Honey-Glazed Nectarines with Ricotta and Amaretti, 202
- Ice Cream with Chocolate Sauce and Peanut Brittle, 193
- Masala Shrimp Kebabs with Yogurt Sauce, 93
- Moroccan Lamb Chops with Spiced Chickpeas, 73
- Muesli with Apricots and Almonds, 155
- Pepper Steak and Watercress Sandwiches, 169
- Peppered Tuna with Lemongrass Vinaigrette, 88
- Pesto Chicken and Mushroom Kebabs, 79
- Polenta Pizza Margherita, 57
- Pork Pitas with Chutney Sauce, 119

- Salmon with Coconut-Tomato Sauce, 42
- Soba Chicken Noodle Bowl, 81
- Spicy Thai Crab Rolls with Basil, 141
- Strawberry-Mascarpone Toasts, 185
- Sun-Dried Tomato and Basil Stuffed Pork, 22
- Thai Shrimp Summer Rolls, 45
- Tofu, Broccolini, and Cashew Stir-Fry, 101
- Turkey Sausage, Tomato, and Basil Pizza, 86
- Warm Caramel Pineapple with Raspberries, 190
- Warm Coconut Rice with Mango, 198
- Warm Tuna, Butter Bean, and Pasta Salad, 139
- Weeknight Beef and Vegetable Stew, 64

- Brazilian Chicken with Black Beans and Rice, 32
- Cannoli Cream and Cookies, 194
- Caramelized Onion Risotto with Chickpeas, 99
- Grilled Pork Tenderloin with Chipotle-Peach Glaze, 24
- Korean-Style Steak and Kimchi Wraps, 109
- Lemon-Basil Tofu with Pasta and Zucchini, 53
- Mustard Chicken with Black-Eyed Pea Salad, 124
- Pork Chops with Asian Pineapple Salsa, 116
- Roasted Eggplant and Hummus Tartines, 100
- Salmon and Bok Choy in Thai Curry Broth, 96
- Spiced Pork Chops with Scallion Couscous, 117
- Steak Pizzaiola with Polenta, 111
- Three-Cheese and Tomato Pizzas, 149
- Tilapia with Prosciutto and Artichokes, 90
- Tuna and Penne Salad with Basil and Olives, 41

- Beef and Mushroom Ragu with Polenta, 20
- Beef and Portobello Burgers, 68
- Bowties with Broccoli Pesto, 97
- Buffalo Chicken Burgers with Blue Cheese Dressing, 83
- Chicken and Couscous Salad with Dried Cherries, 160

continued

- Corn and Black Bean Enchilada Casserole, 148
- Crumb-Crusted Scallops with Parmesan Tomatoes, 91
- Dijon-Glazed Chicken and Tomatoes, 76
- Greek Chicken with Peppers and Pasta, 132
- Harissa-Spiced Sirloin with Raisin Couscous, 14
- Hoisin-Glazed Tilapia with Soba Noodles, 138
- Lamb Kebabs with Yogurt-Mint Sauce, 74
- Lemon-Herb Snack Mix, 187
- Pecan-Crusted Chicken with Cilantro Slaw, 30
- Pressure Cooker Pepper Pot Stew, 21
- Pressure Cooker Winter Vegetable and Bean Soup, 50
- Tex-Mex Nacho Scramble, 156
- Turkey Sausage and Cranberry Sandwiches, 163

- Beef Stroganoff Stir-Fry, 66
- Grilled Lamb Koftas with Yogurt-Cilantro Sauce, 27
- Kielbasa with Pasta, Chickpeas, and Spinach, 135
- Smoky Lamb and Lentil Stew, 28

- Chicken and Tomatillo Soft Tacos, 82
- Pan-Roasted Salmon with Lentils and Feta, 137
- Thai Beef and Vegetable Curry, 67

- Quick Clam and Roasted Pepper Paella, 140

- Pressure Cooker Moroccan Chicken Stew, 35

Recipes that work with the Simply Filling technique

30 MINUTES

Brazilian Chicken with Black Beans and Rice, 32

Caribbean Chicken and Pineapple Kebabs, 34

Grilled Turkey Cutlets with Watermelon Salsa, 37

Pressure Cooker Winter Vegetable and Bean Soup, 50

20 MINUTES

Grilled "Béarnaise" Chicken, 78

Indian-Spiced Pork with Squash Sauté, 71

Moroccan Lamb Chops with Spiced Chickpeas, 73

Sirloin with Cherry Tomatoes and Basil, 62

15 MINUTES

Chicken and Polenta with Zucchini-Tomato Sauce, 123

Halibut and Asparagus with Tomato Sauce, 142

Lemon Chicken with Arugula and Tomato Salad, 127

Mustard Chicken with Black-Eyed Pea Salad, 124

Rosemary Lamb Chops with Balsamic Tomatoes, 121

Spiced Pork Chops with Scallion Couscous, 117

Warm Tuna, Butter Bean, and Pasta Salad, 139

BONUS 15 MINUTES

Cherry Tomato and Baby Spinach Sauté, 177

Couscous with Chickpeas and Oranges, 172

Lemony Fennel and Radicchio, 180

Sautéed Zucchini and Tomatoes with Cardamom, 178

Smoky Kasha with Scallions, 173

Spicy Bulgur and Carrots with Harissa, 175

Dry and Liquid Measurement Equivalents

If you are converting the recipes in this book to metric measurements, use the following chart as a guide.

TEASPOONS	TABLESPOONS	CUPS	FLUID OUNCES
3 teaspoons	1 tablespoon		½ fluid ounce
6 teaspoons	2 tablespoons	⅛ cup	1 fluid ounce
8 teaspoons	2 tablespoons plus 2 teaspoons	⅙ cup	
12 teaspoons	4 tablespoons	¼ cup	2 fluid ounces
15 teaspoons	5 tablespoons	⅓ cup minus 1 teaspoon	
16 teaspoons	5 tablespoons plus 1 teaspoon	⅓ cup	
18 teaspoons	6 tablespoons	¼ cup plus 2 tablespoons	3 fluid ounces
24 teaspoons	8 tablespoons	½ cup	4 fluid ounces
30 teaspoons	10 tablespoons	½ cup plus 2 tablespoons	5 fluid ounces
32 teaspoons	10 tablespoons plus 2 teaspoons	⅔ cup	
36 teaspoons	12 tablespoons	¾ cup	6 fluid ounces
42 teaspoons	14 tablespoons	1 cup minus 2 tablespoons	7 fluid ounces
45 teaspoons	15 tablespoons	1 cup minus 1 tablespoon	
48 teaspoons	16 tablespoons	1 cup	8 fluid ounces

VOLUME	
¼ teaspoon	1 milliliter
½ teaspoon	2 milliliters
1 teaspoon	5 milliliters
1 tablespoon	15 milliliters
2 tablespoons	30 milliliters
3 tablespoons	45 milliliters
¼ cup	60 milliliters
⅓ cup	80 milliliters
½ cup	120 milliliters
⅔ cup	160 milliliters
¾ cup	175 milliliters
1 cup	240 milliliters
1 quart	950 milliliters

LENGTH	
1 inch	25 millimeters
1 inch	2.5 centimeters

WEIGHT	
1 ounce	30 grams
¼ pound	120 grams
½ pound	240 grams
1 pound	480 grams

OVEN TEMPERATURE			
250°F	120°C	400°F	200°C
275°F	140°C	425°F	220°C
300°F	150°C	450°F	230°C
325°F	160°C	475°F	250°C
350°F	180°C	500°F	260°C
375°F	190°C	525°F	270°C

Note: Measurement of less than ⅛ teaspoon is considered a dash or a pinch. Metric measurements are approximate.